HOW TO IMPROVE YOUR STUDY SKILLS

Marcia J. Coman

Kathy L. Heavers

D1400662

VGM Career Horizons
a division of *NTC Publishing Group*
Lincolnwood, Illinois USA

Acknowledgments

Grateful acknowledgment is made to the following for permission to reprint copyrighted materials:

Ward Cramer, for *Speedreading for Better Grades* excerpts. Copyright 1978, J. Weston Walch, Publisher.

Employment & Training Administration, U.S. Employment Service, Washington, DC 20210, for "Merchandising Your Job Talents"

P. Patrick Hooley, for "Creating Successful Study Habits"

Houghton-Mifflin Company, for dictionary excerpts. Copyright © 1983 by Houghton Mifflin Company. Reprinted by permission from *The American Heritage Dictionary*, paperback edition.

Fred Matheny, for "Cycling's Risks." From Fred Matheny, *Beginning Bicycle Racing*, copyright 1983.

Judy McKenna and Carole J. Makela, for "It's Your Money—Managing Credit," Colorado State University–Cooperative Extension, Fort Collins, CO.

Kendall Slee, for "One Night in the Woods"

Trans World Airlines, for "TWA Flight Schedule." Reprinted by permission of Trans World Airlines, Inc.

Mary Lael Van Riper, for "Mary Had a Little Lamb"

H. W. Wilson Company, for *Readers' Guide* excerpts. *Readers' Guide to Periodical Literature*, July 1988 issue, copyright © 1988 by The H. W. Wilson Company. Material reproduced by permission of the publisher.

Photos: Steve Gottlieb, pp. 22, 28, 78, 97, 101, 133, 180; Larry Risser, Unit Openers and pp. 3, 7, 17, 26, 40, 43, 52, 63, 64, 70, 75, 108, 115, 119, 146, 147, 152, 155, 168, 171, 178; Solveig C. Robinson, p. 127

Illustrations: Sandra Burton

Designer: Linda Snow Shum

1992 Printing

Contents

UNIT ONE
Getting Started 2

UNIT TWO
Developing Study Skills 6

UNIT THREE
Note Taking 20

UNIT FOUR
Taking Tests 34

UNIT FIVE
Improving Your Understanding 56

UNIT SIX
Increasing Speed 78

UNIT SEVEN
Skimming and Scanning 104

UNIT EIGHT
Using the Dictionary 132

UNIT NINE
Exploring the Library/Media Center 145

UNIT TEN
Reading for Enjoyment 164

UNIT ELEVEN
Summing It Up .186

Glossary 202

Index 205

Getting Started

*D*o you know that when you take a test, you are not only being tested on your knowledge of a subject, but on your test-taking techniques, as well? Many students feel nervous about taking tests, and their anxiety makes it difficult for them to concentrate or remember.

After you study a subject, do you find you can't recall much about it? If this has happened to you, you'll be eager to learn the simple techniques that will help you study more efficiently and effectively. *Where, when*, and *how* you study affect your ability to recall information.

When you take notes, do you try to include only the important things, or do you race to record everything your instructor says? In class, some students scribble away in their notebooks, only to find later that they can't decipher what they wrote.

Most people would like to be able to read faster and understand and remember material better. Are you a slow reader, or do you read everything from paperback mysteries to your science textbook at the same rate? Could you read at speeds of 1,000 words per minute or more?

Suppose you have just been given an assignment involving research. Where do you begin? Because they don't know how to use them, many people think of the dictionary as a bulky book of words and their meanings and the newspaper as a collection of comics, sports, and classified ads. But these resources, as well as the media center library, are great sources of information we all need. We have to *learn* how to use them well.

Each year the American College Test Program publishes a survey of students in which approximately 35 percent respond that they need additional help in reading and 45 percent request further development of their study skills. Would you place yourself in these percentages?

Information now being published predicts that the average person will have to retrain for a new job five times during his or her working life span, and that 56 percent of the jobs people will hold in the year 2005 do not even exist today. With so much change in your future, skills you can acquire in school involve how to learn, how to study, how to research, and how to read with more speed and better comprehension.

This book addresses each of these skills in very special ways. Written by instructors, and used, tested, and revised by students and instructors over a period of several years, *How to Improve Your Study Skills* is a compilation of techniques that people have discovered *really work*.

We believe you will find that you can use these basic skills every day to improve your abilities in all the areas we have discussed. And we believe that you will find the materials in this book easy to adapt to your particular learning style and reading and study habits.

Remember: Some of the greatest and most beneficial skills you can acquire—the ones that will help you throughout your life—are skills that focus on the abilities to learn, study, research, and read with appropriate speed and comprehension. This text was written to help you develop and sharpen those essential skills.

Take time to introduce yourself and to get to know the other students.

Activity 1-1
Introductions

You have enrolled in this class because you want to improve your study skills. So, how do you go about it? The activities in Unit 1 are the way to start, because they will help to acquaint you with your instructor and your classmates. You can ask questions about what you will be doing in class and how it will help you. At the same time, you will learn what your instructor's expectations are for the class.

As you, your fellow students, and your instructor continue your discussion, you may be surprised to notice that you feel more prepared and comfortable already in this new environment.

Your instructor may begin by introducing himself or herself and asking you to do the same. Besides giving your name, mention your year in school and any hobbies, activities, or part-time jobs you have. After you know a little bit about your instructor and the other students, naturally you will want to learn more about the class itself. Throughout the class, there will be many opportunities like this one for you to take part in discussions developing your interpersonal communication skills.

Activity 1–2
Interest Inventory

You have characteristics and interests and habits that make you special. Sometimes, writing about yourself helps you become more aware of your talents and uniqueness. For example, why are you taking this class? In what subjects are you strongest? In what areas would you like to improve? Are you the reader you would like to be? Knowing the answers to questions such as these could help you to become a better student. Your answers will also aid your instructor in identifying your strong and your not-so-strong areas.

On a separate sheet of paper, answer the following questions in the Interest Inventory. When you finish completing it, you'll know yourself a little better.

Interest Inventory

1. What do you like to do with your spare time?

2. What do you consider as career possibilities?

3. List your favorite subjects at school.

4. List your least favorite subjects.

5. Imagine a free day. What would you do with it?

6. If you could be anyone in the world, who would you be?

7. What is the title of the best book you've ever read?

8. What is (are) your favorite type(s) of book(s)?

9. During the past year have you read any books for pleasure? How many? List their titles.

10. Do you read the newspaper (or part of one) daily? If you do, which one(s)? Which part(s)?

11. Do you read comic books? If you do, which one(s)?

12. What are your favorite TV programs?

13. Are you employed part-time? Describe what you do during the week from 4:00 PM until you go to bed.

14. Would you describe yourself as a leisure time reader? Do you read frequently, sometimes, or never?

15. Do you have a library card? Do you use the library often, sometimes, or rarely?

16. How could this class promote your own reading for enjoyment?

17. Is there specific information you need on reading or study skills right now? If so, what is it?

18. On a separate sheet of paper, reconstruct a class schedule like the one shown below and fill it out for the classes in which you are currently enrolled.

Hour	Name of Class	Instructor	Level of Difficulty for You Most Difficult=1, Least Difficult=5
1			
2			
3			
4			
5			
6			
7			
8			
9			

19. What are your plans after graduating from high school? (College, vocational or trade school, armed forces, job?)

Activity 1-3
Reading Assessment

When you complete your Interest Inventory, your instructor may wish to give an assessment test to determine your actual reading skills. This test will measure your vocabulary, reading comprehension, and reading speed. Don't get nervous; you cannot fail an assessment. This test merely pinpoints your personal starting place on the road to improving your reading and study skills.

Developing Study Skills

DEVELOP (di věl' əp), v. To evolve to a more complete state

STUDY (stud'e) n. The pursuit of knowledge

SKILLS (skĭl) n. Proficiency, expertness

Were you ever taught *how* to study? Instructors often assume that students beyond grade school know and use good study techniques. You may know some people who seem to be able to do more in less time, and get good grades besides. How do they do it?

In this unit you will learn some simple techniques that good students consider most important when studying. Now you can discover some of their secrets.

Activity 2–1
Previewing Your Textbook

Learn to *preview your textbook*, and you'll be on your way to becoming a better student. By spending no more than five minutes the first day of class to preview each of your new texts, you can determine what material will be covered in the book, how familiar you are with the material, and how difficult the material will be for you. In addition, you will discover the book's format and the aids included to make your job as a student easier.

You can practice the technique now. Using a separate sheet of paper and this textbook, answer the following questions. Your answers will become your five-minute preview of this text.

1. List the title of the text.

2. List the author(s).

3. What is the text's most recent copyright date?

Previewing your text-
book makes studying
easier.

4. Read the preface or introduction. Summarize in a few sentences what the book is going to be about.

5. Read the Table of Contents. How many chapters are in the text? How many pages are in the text? List the title of the chapter that sounds most interesting to you.

6. Thumb through the book. Are there pictures? Graphs? Maps? Charts? Illustrations? Questions at the end of the chapters? Pages with a lot of white space?

7. Evaluate the difficulty of the text; how hard do you think this text will be for you to read and understand?

8. Turn to the end of the text. What appendixes does it have?

Activity 2–2
What Is "Previewing"?

Now that you actually have previewed a textbook, read the following article, "How to Preview Your Textbook." Using a separate sheet of paper, start a section of notes and entitle this section "Study Skills—Previewing Your Textbook." First, list the seven steps in previewing your textbook. Then, in your own words, answer the questions:

1. How do you preview your text?

2. What is the value of previewing your text?

How to Preview Your Textbook

The difference between being a good student or being a poor one sometimes hinges on whether you know how to study. There are some

very basic study techniques that require only a short amount of time to learn, but that result in tremendous benefits. Previewing your text is one of these techniques.

Previewing your text involves looking at a book before a class begins to determine what the text contains. This process will take no more than five minutes, but in that amount of time you will gain much useful information. Your preview can reveal what material will be covered in the book and in the class, how familiar you are with that material, and how difficult that material will be for you to read and understand. You will be able to determine the following: the format of the book; the location of the study aids, pictures, charts, and graphs used throughout; and your level of interest in the material. Equipped with this information, you are a more informed and prepared student already, and you will save yourself study time later on.

The first step in previewing your text is to look at the title, author, and date of publication, or copyright date. The copyright date is important because it not only tells you how current the information is, it also tells you how popular the book has been. A book that has been printed and reprinted several times is usually a very popular one.

Next, read the preface or introduction. It usually discusses the scope of the book and explains why the authors wrote it.

Third, find the table of contents and read the chapter titles, main headings, and subheadings included within. Turn these into questions so that you can read with a purpose to find the answers.

Then, flip through the book, looking at any charts, pictures, captions, and graphs. These items provide additional information about the subject and also affect your interest in reading the text.

Fifth, evaluate the difficulty of the material. How much do you already know about the subject? How much does it interest you? Is the print large or small? How much white space does a typical page have? Are there many pictures, charts, graphs, and illustrations? These factors all determine the level of difficulty of the text and the amount of material you will have to read.

Next, know your purpose for reading the text. Are you required to read it for class? Will the teacher test you on its contents? Or is it just a supplement to the teacher's notes? Knowing your purpose is crucial in determining how and at what rate you should read the text.

Last, go to the back of the book to see what study aids are included. Does the text include a glossary of words and their meanings to help you with vocabulary? Is there an index listing names, events, terms, and the pages on which the items can be found? Better yet, does the appendix have solutions to problems you have been asked to solve? Obviously, all these materials will help you as you read the text, *if you know they are there*. If you don't spend time previewing your text, however, you may not discover them.

Activity 2–3
Study Setting Worksheet

Take a look at where you study, how you study, and what your "study center" consists of. How strong is your power of concentration in this environment? It may surprise you to learn that your study center, your study environment, and your method of studying directly affect your concentration and comprehension.

For a few minutes, think about your own study situation and environment. Then, on a separate sheet of paper, list the conditions that make it hard for you to concentrate. Be honest—no one will deduct points if your study area is a disaster! Be sure to leave room to jot down later your solutions to any problem conditions.

STUDY SETTING WORKSHEET

Conditions That Make It Hard For Me to Concentrate	Ways I Can Improve Those Conditions

Activity 2–4
Tips on Concentration

Read the following article, "Tips on Concentration." Then, add to your notes on study skills at least seven tips for improving your study environment, study techniques, and concentration.

Tips on Concentration

Think about your usual study environment. Are you sprawled on your bed with the stereo blaring, books and papers scattered around you? Are you trying not to spill the Coke when you retrieve that elusive pencil? Or is it, perhaps, flat on the floor on your stomach, in front of the TV, with the dog licking your ear and your brothers playing "invaders from space" nearby? If this sounds at all familiar, you may find concentration—or the lack of it—one of your biggest hindrances to effective studying.

"But," you ask, "how can I concentrate better?" The following tips have been gathered from students who have learned to do so.

Study in the same place every day. Psychologically, this establishes a pattern that your brain will respond to automatically when you settle down in that spot day after day. When your study place is your bed, the desire to study is in conflict with the desire to sleep, which often causes problems for many students.

In spite of what you may think, studying in a quiet place is more beneficial than being surrounded by music or other noise. From experience, you know you can learn to block certain sounds from your consciousness, such as the exasperated tone of your mother's voice calling, or the rumble of passing traffic. But having a quiet area is critical, because comprehension rates zoom downward in direct relationship to the amount of sound in your environment. Some experts assert comprehension can actually be cut in half!

Since your primary occupation at this time is that of student, make your "office" a study center. Gather together all the equipment you need to do your work. Face a blank wall if possible; don't let distractions creep in to break your concentration. After all, this is where you do your work.

Good lighting and ventilation are primary requirements when you set up your study area. Invest in a desk lamp that will eliminate glare and uneven lighting. Open the window a crack, even in chilly weather, to fend off stuffiness and the yawns that quickly follow.

Have a working surface that is large enough for your needs, and clear it of any clutter. Be sure to provide room for the supplies you need— perhaps just a shoe box on the floor beside your working area.

Remember, too, that your eyes will see more easily and become less tired if you prop your book up at a 30-degree angle, rather than leaving it flat on the desk top. Either hold your book at an angle, use other texts as a support, or build a book rest.

You will concentrate better if you have only one task before you at a time; too many tasks may overwhelm you. Always complete one task before beginning another. Avoid the urge to get something to eat or to call a friend. Instead, use these well-known stalling techniques as rewards for yourself when you have completed a task. With a definite plan of attack, you'll finish with all your assignments sooner.

Learning to concentrate is hard work, but the payoff is better grades. Good students have mastered this skill. You can too!

Activity 2–5
Solutions to Study Setting Problems

Now, consult your list of conditions that make it hard for you to concentrate (Activity 2–3) and think of some practical solutions to your problems. List the solution opposite the corresponding problem.

For the next week, put your solutions into practice. See how successful you are, and be persistent. Remember, it takes time to change habits. Then evaluate what did and did not work for you. Decide what permanent changes you can make to improve your study setting.

Activity 2–6
Where Does Your Time Go?

It seems we never have enough time to accomplish what we want to. Are you good at disciplining yourself to use your time wisely? Each day, how do you spend the sixteen hours you are not in school?

Consider the fact that the average kindergarten graduate has already seen more than 5,000 hours of television by age five or six. That is more time than it takes to get a bachelor's degree from college! How much time have you spent in front of the television? Perhaps you don't realize where your time really does go.

On the other hand, you might know someone who *always* comes to class prepared, who studies sufficiently for *every* exam, who carefully prepares *each* written assignment, and who comprehensively reads the text material. Do you envy that person as you scramble before class to get your work done, however haphazardly? If only you had more control of your time . . . .

Tracking Your Time

To help you pinpoint what you really do with your time, on a separate sheet of paper make a chart like the following and complete it according to your schedule for *one typical day in your school week.*

Start with the time you generally awaken, and continue to identify how you spend your time throughout the day, right up until when you usually go to bed. Include hours spent dressing, eating, traveling to and from school, attending classes, visiting, exercising, working, studying, watching TV, talking on the phone, sleeping, and so on. Make sure your log represents a twenty-four-hour period.

Time	Activity	Time	Activity

Now answer on your own paper the following summary questions:

1. How much time do you use to eat and dress?

2. How much time do you spend traveling to and from school?

3. How many hours do you attend classes?

4. How much time is used for exercising?

5. How much time is spent watching TV, visiting, or just relaxing?

6. How many hours do you work at a part-time job?

7. How many hours do you sleep?

Activity 2–7
Controlling Your Time

What did you discover when you used the chart to determine how you spend your time? Many people feel that they waste time, but they don't know how to correct the problem. The following article, "Tips for Control of Your Time," is written to give you some time-budgeting suggestions. Read it, and add to your notes on Study Skills one key idea from each paragraph.

Tips for Control of Your Time

Controlling your time is somewhat like learning to budget your money. At first, the money always runs out before the month ends, but with practice and planning, your money management skills increase. Just so with budgeting your time!

If you want to be in control of your time, a plan is vital. Your survival depends on it. Think about the things you must accomplish and decide approximately how much time you need to do them. Write these down; they provide a guide or budget for spending your hours and minutes.

Are you most alert in the morning or at night? This is important to know, because you should plan your study time accordingly. You will accomplish far more if you study when your concentration abilities are sharp.

Think about your study sequence. Hardest assignments to easiest? Alternating activities such as reading, then drawing a map, then back to reading? You may prefer the first-things-first method, finishing the most important projects before any of the others, and risking the possibility of leaving some things undone. Each of the study sequences mentioned here is used by successful students. As personalities vary, so do study sequences.

You'll be pleased to know that you *should* allow yourself breaks as you study. Some research suggests taking breaks of approximately ten minutes every hour. The best time to do so, of course, is between tasks. Breaks rest your mind and your eyes.

If you like structure, set up your time budget in an exact time frame. If, on the other hand, you dislike rigid time limits, plan your sequence without specific time allotments. Either approach can be successful, but

remember that a time budget, like a budget of dollars and cents, must be somewhat flexible. It is sometimes hard to judge how long a task will take. If you can't meet the time requirement that you have allowed, revise your schedule. Because unexpected things come up, try to have some time in reserve, if possible.

If your out-of-school life is always in a state of chaos, devote a few minutes daily to sequencing your tasks. By having some plan, whether it be closely structured or more loosely organized, you will know the satisfaction that comes with gaining more control of your time.

Activity 2–8
Budgeting Your Time

Can you see from Activities 2–6 and 2–7 any areas where you might be able to adjust your present schedule in order to use your time more efficiently? List them on a separate sheet of paper.

Then create another chart like the one in Activity 2–6 for a schedule in which you will plan ahead. For the next week you are to create a new budget for your time. Keep in mind the best ways to use your time; your goal is to be more efficient.

At the end of one week, evaluate your new schedule. Did you succeed in using your time more to your advantage? If you found you were more prepared and less rushed, you will probably be eager to make your trial schedule changes permanent.

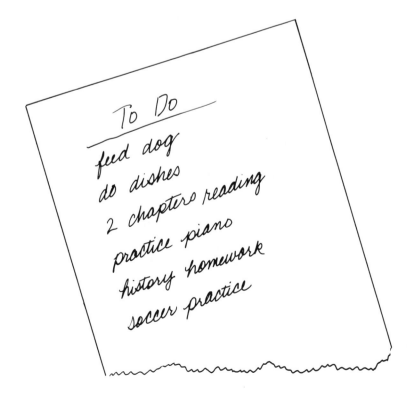

Activity 2–9
Sizing Up Your Instructor

"That instructor doesn't like me." "I can't do anything right in his class." "I never know what to expect in her class." Do you recall making similar remarks? If so, maybe you never ask yourself what your *instructor* expects.

Teachers are as different from one another as you are from your friends. Some are very relaxed in their approach while others rely on lots of structure. Some are very explicit in what they expect from students and what kinds of tests they give. Others may not be so direct.

If you want to learn as much as you can and have the best possible grades, it's your job as a student to understand the expectations of each of your instructors. This process doesn't take long, and it's not difficult either. Use your powers of observation, and if you still aren't sure, *ask* your instructor.

To begin, in the first days of class spend a few minutes thinking about your instructor's expectations regarding the following: your behavior, participation, and note taking; his or her method of grading and testing; and, finally, the appropriate techniques you can use to study for that instructor's class. You will be amazed at the results! Not only will you know how to tailor your studying to each class and its instructor's expectations, you'll earn better grades and waste less time.

Next, select the instructor or class that you find most difficult. Remember, the purpose of this exercise is to guide you through an evaluation of your instructor's expectations about you as a student. Once you determine what those expectations are, you can adjust your efforts accordingly and thus minimize your study time and improve your grade.

On a separate sheet of paper, list the expectations of your instructor, as you understand them, in each of the following areas. Be sure to allow enough room to write.

Instructor's Expectations of My Behavior and Participation:
1. At the beginning of the hour;

2. During the hour;

3. At the end of the hour;

4. In general.

Instructor's Expectations in the Areas of:
1. Note taking;

2. Study techniques;

3. Tests;

4. Grades.

Activity 2–10
Accuracy of Instructor's Expectations

Take your list of perceived expectations (Activity 2–9) to the instructor you selected and ask him or her to read it to see just how accurate you were.

If you were good at predicting what your instructor wants, you're off to a strong start in his or her class. If, on the other hand, you don't yet have a very clear picture of what is expected, ask your instructor specific questions about each area on your expectations list until you understand what he or she wants. Learn now—not after a test. Surprises aren't fun when grades are involved.

```
S  Q        3      R
u  u               Read
r  e
v  s
e  t
y  i               Recite
   o
   n               Review
```

Activity 2–11
The SQ3R Method

An important part of improving your study skills is finding a dependable study technique. Some of you may already have discovered a method that gives you good results, but others may have no system at all . . . and have grades that show it. If you haven't had the opportunity to develop a study technique yet, the SQ3R method may be for you.* On a separate sheet of paper, add notes on SQ3R to your Study Skills information.

SQ3R

As students, most of you know it is not enough to simply read an assignment. The act of reading does not insure that you will remember what you have read. Perhaps you daydream while you read, or maybe you are surrounded by background noise, commotion, or interruptions. In any case, you can't recall a thing about what you just read. Sound familiar?

You need to be an active participant as you read and study. You can do that by practicing a technique that involves you in the learning process—SQ3R. Many of you already use part of the SQ3R technique if you preview material. You carry it even further if, as you read, you try to find answers to questions about the materials. Both the previewing and questioning techniques are important steps in SQ3R, but there is more to it.

---

* SQ3R was developed in 1941 by Francis Robinson; it has become a popular and successful study technique.

S = Survey

The *S* in SQ3R stands for *survey* (or preview). This should already be a familiar term to you. To review, the steps in the survey are simple and take very little time. They are:

1. Look at the title;

2. Read the first paragraph or introduction;

3. Read the first sentence of each of the other paragraphs;

4. Read the last paragraph or conclusion.

The survey step helps you in four ways:

1. You get a glimpse of the contents of the material without having to read every word;

2. You get a feel for your familiarity with the material;

3. You can estimate the amount of time you should set aside for covering the material; and

4. You may actually double your comprehension when you do read the entire selection.

The survey does all this in a matter of minutes!

Q = Question

In order to become actively involved in the actual reading process, you need to read with a purpose in mind. That is, you need to *read to answer questions*. Look to the following sources for questions you can answer as you read:

1. Questions listed at the end of the chapter;

2. Questions provided by your instructor;

3. Headings you turn into questions; and

4. Questions on worksheets, quizzes, or tests.

Knowing the questions *before* you actually read the selection helps you read for a purpose. You will be an involved reader, and your comprehension and retention of the material will be greatly improved. Better yet, after you finish reading the selection, you will find you know the *answers* to the questions you had as you read.

R = Read

Try it. Read the material as an active reader with the goal of answering questions as you go along. You'll be surprised at how much more you'll get out of your reading assignment, and you'll feel good when your reading reveals answers.

Reciting after reading increases your retention of material.

R = Recite

The next step is to *recite* the answers to your questions. Recite aloud to another person or quietly to yourself what you have read. Studies show that students tend to forget as much as 80 percent of what they have learned from reading within two weeks after studying. But when students recited immediately after reading, they forgot only 20 percent during the same time period.

Recite it, and then write it down, if necessary. This is the proof that you understand and comprehend what you have read—that you have been actively involved in the reading process. You know what you have read because you can recite the answers to questions.

R = Review

After a few hours, or even a couple of days, *review* the answers to your questions. This step will keep the material fresh in your mind, and you can retain it and recall it accurately for longer periods of time.

In addition, using the SQ3R method will save you from test anxiety and late-night or all-night crash study sessions, cramming for exams. SQ3R helps you learn and retain the material so you can approach a test with confidence.

Activity 2–12
Practice with SQ3R

Learning anything that is new takes some practice before it feels comfortable; the SQ3R technique for studying is no exception. Start by trying the SQ3R method on a chapter from a textbook that is difficult for you. Use your notes and *think* about what you are doing and why you are doing it.

Next, give yourself a long-term trial with SQ3R. Commit to consciously using this technique for two weeks as you study *one* subject that gives you difficulty. Be conscientious and follow the procedure steps exactly. SQ3R is used successfully by many students—see if it is a technique that will work for you.

Activity 2–13
Unit Review

This is a review of what you have learned in Unit 2 on developing study skills. Try to remember the major points that were covered. On a separate sheet of paper, answer the following questions:

I. Multiple-Choice
    Number your paper from one to five. Place the letter of the correct answer beside the corresponding number.

1. In what order should you study subjects?

    A. Hardest or least interesting to easiest or most interesting
    B. Alternate types of activities
    C. First things first, in order of descending importance
    D. Any of the above

2. What is the benefit of a study budget or time sheet?

    A. Sets immediate goals
    B. Helps concentration because you are working against the clock
    C. Helps resist distractions
    D. All of the above

3. How long should a break be?

    A. Five minutes
    B. Ten minutes
    C. Fifteen minutes
    D. As long as you need it to be

4. What did the article you read say about taking breaks?

    A. They are optional and not really important.
    B. They are a waste of time and should be omitted.
    C. They are absolutely essential, or your concentration will falter.
    D. They should be taken frequently; every thirty minutes is best.

5. Your study schedule should be:

    A. Very rigid. If you do not follow it carefully you'll never develop any self-discipline.
    B. Flexible. You'll become frustrated and easily discouraged if it is too rigid and you can't live up to it.
    C. Quickly disposed of. A study schedule forces you to be too organized and has very little benefit.
    D. Made out for weeks in advance. Careful planning never hurt anyone.

II. Listing

6 to 12. Number your paper from six through twelve. Read the questions carefully, choose **one** of the two questions, and write the correct answers.

    A. List seven tips concerning the setting or environment in which you should study if you wish to get maximum comprehension.

    B. List the seven steps in previewing your text.

13 to 17. List the words represented by the name SQ3R.

III. Short Essay

18. Choose one of the following topics and write your answer in paragraph form.

    A. Describe what is involved in previewing your text and discuss the benefits you found when you previewed three of your texts.

    B. Discuss the value of creating a good study setting, explain the changes you made in your study setting, and conclude by discussing how these changes have helped you improve your concentration.

    C. Explain the steps in SQ3R and discuss how this technique will be beneficial to you.

Note Taking

NOTE (nōt) n. Written record or communication

TAKE (tāk) v. To write down

lmost anyone would agree: Note taking can be a real chore! Some instructors talk so fast, you can't begin to keep up. Others wander from one subject to the next until you can't even remember the points they are trying to make. A fast talker leaves your hand numb from writer's cramp. A disorganized speaker leaves you dizzy with confusion—and with few notes in your notebook. You need a better, more efficient method for taking notes.

Notes and note taking are personal. No two students take notes in the same way, although each is trying to pick out the same main points from a lecture. Whether you consider yourself a skilled or unskilled note taker, your note taking can improve. You can learn to be more flexible and concise.

Unit 3 will give you experience using several methods of taking notes, as well as some shortcuts you can use—regardless of the type of note-taking technique you favor. The exercises in this unit will help you "streamline" your note taking; in other words, they'll help you develop skills that will make it easier to take notes efficiently. And, because you will soon be an efficient note taker, the notes you take will be more useful to you, too.

Activity 3–1
Evaluating Your Present System

This activity lets you evaluate your own note-taking techniques and illustrates a concise method for taking notes in the future. For those of you who have trouble deciding what to include in your notes, practice picking out the main points and subpoints from the material.

Part One

First, read the following selection entitled "Evaluating Your Present System." As you read, use your standard note-taking technique to take notes on a separate sheet of paper. When you finish, compare your notes with those in the answer key at the end of this unit.

Evaluating Your Present System

Lectures given by teachers are fleeting things. The ideas and concepts presented, unless captured on paper by students taking notes, are quickly confused or forgotten. In order to recall a lecture's main points, you must develop good note-taking skills.

First, you have to concentrate on the lecture. You cannot think about your plans for the evening, tomorrow's dance, or your next car repair. Next, you must learn to pick out the speaker's important points and to exclude the insignificant details. To do this, listen for signal words. Third, you should develop a system for taking notes. Many students use an outline form because it is simple and straightforward. Fourth, you need to find ways to streamline your note-taking system. That is, don't miss an important point because you fall behind as you write. Last, you need to review your notes soon after taking them to fill in any additional information and refresh your memory on the major points.

Part Two

Compare the notes you took with the outline provided in the answer key at the end of this unit. How did you do?

1. Did you use complete sentences? Complete sentences are a waste of time. Be brief, using only key words.

2. Did you use an outline form, or any form at all? Would you describe your notes as clear or confusing?

3. Did you capture the main point and all the subpoints? Signal words in this selection such as "First, . . . next, . . . third, . . . fourth, . . . and last" should help you recognize the subpoints.

4. Did you use any abbreviations or shortcuts while taking your notes? If not, you'll want to focus on streamlining your note taking.

Activity 3–2
Note-taking Questionnaire

This activity uses a survey to give you insight into your thoughts about note taking, your individual note-taking practices, and your weaker areas in note taking. Take a minute to complete the survey that follows. Your responses will help you gain the most from this unit by emphasizing specific goals for you.

On a separate sheet of paper, number from one to ten. Leave enough room to make comments for each question.

Note-taking Questionnaire

1. When do you take notes? In class? While studying?

2. Do you find it difficult to take notes while studying? If so, why?

3. Do you ever borrow notes from someone else? If so, are they easier or harder to use than your own?

4. Do you find it difficult to take notes in class? If so, why?

5. Do you write complete sentences when you take notes?

6. List your instructors who expect you to take notes.

7. Do you take notes in those instructors' classes?

8. Do you have trouble picking out main ideas from material?

9. Do you use any shortcuts in taking notes? If so, what are they?

10. Do you feel that taking notes or not taking notes affects the grade you earn?

No two students take notes in the same way. What's important is to find the method that works best for you.

Activity 3–3
Outlining

The first note-taking technique presented in this unit is outlining, the most widely used method of taking notes. Outlining provides you with a well-organized set of notes to study from because it forces you to seek out the main idea and to recognize supporting details. You eliminate other unnecessary information. Once mastered, outlining can be a valuable tool for making you a better student.

Activity 3–3 introduces you to the basics of outlining. It focuses on recognizing main ideas from paragraphs and writing them in proper outline form. Once you have completed this activity, you will have a good understanding of what outlining involves.

If you are not new to outlining, sharpen your skills by reviewing the technique. To help you practice, your instructor may want to provide additional exercises.

Number from one to seven on a separate sheet of paper, leaving room for your comments. Read "The Basics of Outlining" as you follow these directions carefully:

1. Read the first two paragraphs in the article.

2. Answer Questions 1 to 4.

3. Read the next paragraph.

4. Answer Questions 5 to 6.

5. Read the following two paragraphs.

6. Answer Question 7.

7. Read the remainder of the selection and compare your answers to those at the end of the chapter.

The Basics of Outlining

```
I. Topic Sentence
  A. Major Point
    1. Subpoint
      a. detail
```

One of the most important skills for you to develop early in your school career is that of taking notes in an organized manner. In many classes note taking is required. Learning to take organized notes is essential because information is more easily remembered if it is structured when written down.

One of the first steps toward developing an organized note-taking system is being able to recognize the author's main idea; that is, you must clearly understand the point or central thought the author is communicating. That main idea is the topic sentence, and all the other sentences in the paragraph help to support it.

---

1. In Paragraph One, what is the main idea or topic sentence?

2. Where in the paragraph is the main idea or topic sentence located?

3. Find the main idea or topic sentence in Paragraph Two.

4. Where is it located?

You will discover that a paragraph's main idea or topic sentence may be found in a number of different positions in the paragraph. Most frequently, it is the first sentence of the paragraph; the author wants to begin with his or her main idea and use all the other sentences to develop that main idea. The second most frequent location for the topic sentence is the last sentence of the paragraph. By placing the main idea at the end, the author can present a number of details first and then tie them together or sum them up with the topic sentence. Sometimes the main idea may be stated in the first sentence and restated in the last sentence. And occasionally, the main idea may be sandwiched somewhere between the first and last sentences, or split between two sentences. Finally, the topic sentence may be missing altogether! Obviously, topic sentences that are the first or last sentences of a paragraph will be easiest to find. Locating those floating in the middle of a paragraph or split between sentences takes practice.

---

5. On your paper set up the outline form shown below:

I.

   A.
   B.
   C.
   D.
   E.
   F.

What is the main idea or topic sentence in the previous paragraph? Write it beside Roman numeral I.

6. What are the six major points in the previous paragraph? Using the capital letters A through F, list each one.

One of the most widely used methods of note taking—the outline—is preferred by many students because its format follows a specific structure and is concise. Notes taken in this manner are well organized and easily remembered.

---

7. On a separate sheet of paper, copy the outline form shown below:

I.

   A.
   B.
   C.
   D.

Write the main idea for the previous paragraph beside Roman numeral I and the major points beside the capital letters A through D.

Because outlines have specific structures, as mentioned above, you'll find outlining an easy technique to learn. Always write the main idea or topic sentence of a paragraph beside a Roman numeral. Then list each of the major points—those that provide information about the topic—beside a capital letter. Subpoints describe the major points and are listed beside numbers. Finally, supporting details that define, explain, give examples of, give proofs of, or give opinions about the subtopics are placed next to lowercase letters. The paragraph's ideas are thus placed in order of importance. Look at the following example:

I. Main idea or topic sentence

   A. Major points providing information about the topic

      1. Subpoints that describe the major points

         a. Supporting details for the subpoints

Now check your answers for questions one through seven with the answers given at the end of this unit. How accurate are your outlines?

Activity 3-4
More Practice with Outlining

Now that you are familiar with outlining, try your hand at outlining the main ideas and major points in "Paragraph One" and "Paragraph Two."

As you read "Paragraph One" and "Paragraph Two," take notes on a separate sheet of paper keeping in mind three goals as you write:

1. Your notes should be clear and concise.

2. Your notes should include the paragraphs' main ideas and major points.

3. Your notes should use shortcuts, like abbreviations, technical symbols, and personal shorthand.

Take steps to keep your mind from wandering. Don't sit in one position too long—from time to time, stretch to stay alert.

Paragraph One

There are three reasons for learning to take good notes. First, note taking helps you pay attention. While you are writing, you are concentrating, and your mind wanders less. You stay with the subject. Second, note taking helps you remember. In their book *Note Taking Made Easy*, Judi Kesselman-Turkel and Franklynn Peterson state that note taking is a muscle activity, and that our muscles "remember" better than our heads. They give as an example a sixty-eight-year-old man who climbed on a bike for the first time in forty years and, after a few shaky starts, was able to ride off down to the corner. Third, note taking helps you organize ideas. You learn to sort out and write down the main points and subpoints in an organized fashion.

Paragraph Two

In order to keep your mind from wandering when taking notes, there are several steps you can take. First, you can choose your seat carefully. Sit in one of the first few rows, away from distracting doorways and windows. Next, avoid friends, especially friends who capture your attention when you should be listening. In addition, avoid thinking of personal matters. Keep your thoughts on what the speaker is saying and not on your affairs outside of class. Last, stay awake and alert. Take your coat or sweater off if you're too warm, and sit up, with your pen held ready to write. You need to be an active listener.

Now compare your notes with the answers at the end of this unit. How well do your notes match those outlines?

Activity 3–5
Signal Words

In this activity, you will continue to improve your note-taking skill and efficiency. Begin by reviewing your outlines from Activities 3–1, 3–3, and 3–4, and add three new note-taking terms to your vocabulary: *signal words, full signals*, and *half signals.*

Signal words are extremely helpful tools for picking out important details. They serve as flags to indicate main points in sentences or paragraphs. There are two types of signal words: full signals and half signals.

Full signals are obvious flags; they are words such as "the first, the second, the third . . . ."

Half signals are less obvious; they are words such as "the next, the last, in summary, therefore . . . ."

After writing these terms and their definitions in your notes, look back at "More Practice with Outlining" (Activity 3–4) and list on a separate sheet of paper the full signals used in "Paragraph One" and "Paragraph Two." Can you find any half signals? List them. Check your answers with those at the end of this unit.

Activity 3–6
Patterning

In Activity 3–6 you will learn when and how to use the patterning method of note taking. You may discover that you are already using patterning to write flowcharts in your biology, math, or computer lab classes. Sometimes concepts are clearer and information is easier to remember when drawn as a picture rather than written as an outline. In addition, when it's time to review, simple diagrams are easy to understand.

On a separate sheet of paper, practice the patterning method of note taking by drawing three generations of your own family tree. Choose either your mother's side or your father's side of the family and by listing your grandparents' names at the top of your paper. Below their names, list the names of their children (your parent, aunts, and uncles). At the bottom of your family tree, add your own name, as well as the names of your brothers, sisters, and cousins. The basic shape of your three-generation family tree pattern will look like the one following, with variations, of course, based on the number of children in each generation.

—————

————— ————— —————

————— ————— ————— ————— ————— —————

Can you think of any other classes besides the three previously mentioned in which it would be best for you to take notes using the patterning method?

Activity 3–7
Listing

In Activity 3–7, the focus is on listing, a third method of note taking that is extremely straightforward. Listing is an appropriate form of note taking for such classes as history, when dates and important events must be learned, or classes that involve a lot of vocabulary terms and definitions.

When you use this method in class, listen carefully as your instructor lectures, and then build your list. If your source of information is the text or other printed material rather than your instructor's lecture, read carefully and be guided by signal words and key phrases.

To give you practice, your instructor may read a paragraph in class, asking you to use listing to take notes. If he or she does not do this, set up your own notes by listing the important events coming up for you this week. Begin with a heading such as "Events" and follow with a numbered list.

Events
　1.
　2.
　3.
　4.

Were you aware that you really do use three methods for taking notes: outlining, patterning, and listing? Did you realize that different subjects require different note-taking techniques?

Outlining and listing are helpful techniques for taking notes from textbooks.

Activity 3–8
Margin Notes

In addition to outlining, patterning, and listing, you need to know another time-saving method for note taking. However, you can use this method *only* when you own your text or are allowed to write on the material on which you must take notes. If writing in the book or on the material itself is permitted, you can take *margin notes*.

When you use margin notes as your form of note taking, you write down key points in the margin of your book as you read. Margin notes are convenient, providing you with a sufficient set of notes for reviewing at test time.

To practice taking margin notes, choose a set of notes from one of your other classes. Notes from a history, geography, or literature class would work well, as would notes from any other class where the information is fairly detailed. In the margin of your notes, beside the major points, write one to four key words that identify those major points. Now try looking at your margin notes as cues and reciting the major points they represent. Do you see what an important review technique taking margin notes can be at exam time?

Activity 3–9
Highlighting

A fifth method of note taking is highlighting. A highlighter is a marking pen available where school supplies are sold. It allows you to highlight (draw a line over) any key words or phrases you wish to note or emphasize. The ink of the highlighter is light enough to read through.

As a note-taking technique, highlighting saves you writing time and emphasizes key information to review as you study for a test. The obvious disadvantage, of course, is that you must own your own book or other written material in order to use the method.

To practice highlighting, use the highlighter marking pen to draw a line through (or identify) the most important points in a set of your notes—the points your instructor might include on your next test. You'll probably agree it is much easier to study from a set of highlighted notes, than from notes in which every word seems to be as important as the next one.

Activity 3–10
Streamlining

Now that you have five methods of note taking to draw from, let's look at some methods of making note taking easier for you. Do you feel as if you are writing a book as you try to keep up with your instructor's lecture? If so, you need to learn some shortcuts—some ways to streamline your note taking.

As you read "Streamline Your Note Taking," take notes on each of the streamlining techniques. Then, to help you remember what you have read, illustrate each technique with at least three of your own examples.

Streamline Your Note Taking

When you think of streamlining your note taking, you probably think of taking shortcuts such as writing abbreviations in your notes whenever possible. Here are some abbreviations you may already be using:

subj. for *subject*   dept. for *department*

Nov. for *November*   assn. for *association*

But there are more ways you can streamline your note taking. Other practical techniques and examples are listed below:

1. **Leave periods off abbreviations.**
   ex for *example*   no for *number*
   st for *street*   dif for *different*

2. **Use common symbols.**
   & for *and*   + for *plus* or *positive*
   × for *times (multiplication)*   # for *number*

3. **Eliminate vowels.**
   If you are unfamiliar with conventional shorthand, the no-vowel system may save you when you have an instructor who has a very rapid speaking style. Try to read the following set of notes taken using the no-vowel technique:

   Ths prgrph ws wrttn n th "n vwl" nd th "bbrvtd" tchnq.
   Nt ll stdnts lk 2 tk nts ths wy, bt t wrks wll 4 sm. f y
   cn rd ths, y ndrstnd th mssg.

4. **Use word beginnings.**
   Many of you use this technique when you abbreviate.
   intro for *introduction*   com for *committee*
   info for *information*   rep for *representative*

5. **Add "s" to abbreviations to form plurals.**
   exs for *examples*   abbs for *abbreviations*
   mos for *months*   yrs for *years*

6. **Use personal shorthand.**
   Make up abbreviations that are meaningful to you. They need not make sense to other people; if you understand them and they save you time, they are valuable. Did you, for example, use *NT* anywhere in this unit instead of note taking?
   w/ for *with*   4 for *four* or *for*
   w/o for *without*   B4 for *before*

Activity 3–11
Unit Review

On a separate sheet of paper, complete the following to see if you can recall the major points presented in Unit 3.

I. True–False
    Number your paper from one to ten. Write *true* if the statement is true; write *false* if the statement is false.

    1. In order to take good notes, you must concentrate on your instructor's lecture. To do this, you might have to choose a seat away from friends.

    2. It is important to review notes soon after taking them.

    3. Good notes include all the important points, but they also include some unimportant points.

    4. You should choose one system of note taking and stick to that; it is never necessary to use more than one system.

    5. In taking notes, you look for the main ideas, which are the points the author is trying to make.

    6. The main idea appears in only one position in the paragraph; you will always find it in the first sentence.

    7. Note taking is a muscle activity; the muscles you use as you write help you remember the material.

    8. Signal words may or may not help you in taking notes.

    9. "First, second, third," and so on are called *half signals*.

    10. To use margin notes or highlighting as your note-taking techniques, you have to own your textbook.

II. Five Methods of Note Taking
    Number from eleven to fifteen. Briefly explain or illustrate with a drawing the five methods of note taking.

    11. Outlining

    12. Patterning

    13. Listing

    14. Taking margin notes

    15. Highlighting

III. Listing
    Number from sixteen to thirty. List five ways to streamline your note taking and give two examples of each.

    16 to 18. First streamlining technique and two examples.

    19 to 21. Second streamlining technique and two examples.

    22 to 24. Third streamlining technique and two examples.

    25 to 27. Fourth streamlining technique and two examples.

    28 to 30. Fifth streamlining technique and two examples.

IV. Short Essay

31. Describe the method of note taking you find the most useful and explain why it is your preference.

32. Explain what you found to be the most valuable information in this unit and how knowing it will help you.

Appendix
Answers for Activities 3–1, 3–3, 3–4, and 3–5

Activity 3–1: Evaluating Your Present System

I. Need to develop good N T skills

A. Concentrate on lecture

B. Pick out imp. pts./exclude unimp. pts.

C. Develop system

D. Streamline N T so imp. pts. not omitted

E. Review notes

Activity 3–3: Outlining

1. Main idea: "One of the most important skills for you to develop early in your school career is that of taking notes in an organized manner."

2. Location: first sentence

3. Main idea: "One of the first steps toward developing an organized note-taking system is being able to recognize the author's main idea."

4. Location: first sentence

5. Main idea: I. Main idea or topic sentence found in a number of positions

6. Major points: A. first sentence
B. last sentence
C. first and last sentences
D. between first and last sentences
E. split—part in one sentence and part in another
F. not stated at all

7. Main idea: I. Most widely used method: the outline
Major points: A. Format is specific structure
B. It's concise
C. Notes well organized
D. Notes easily remembered

Activity 3–4: More Practice with Outlining

Paragraph One

I. Three reasons for good notes

    A. Helps pay attention

    B. Helps remember

    C. Helps organize ideas

Paragraph Two

I. Steps to keep mind from wandering

    A. Choose seat carefully

    B. Avoid friends

    C. Avoid personal matters

    D. Stay awake and alert

Activity 3–5: Signal Words

Full Signals, Paragraph One: *First; Second; Third*

Full Signals, Paragraph Two: *First*

Half Signals, Paragraph Two: *Next; In addition; Last*

Taking Tests

TAKING (tāk'ing), v. To determine through measurement or observation

TEST (tĕst), n. A series of questions or problems designed to determine knowledge or comprehension

hat words come into your mind when "tests" are mentioned? Success or failure? A's or F's? Do you grow numb with panic and dread the thought of a marathon study session late at night? Maybe you feel calm and confident and look forward to doing well. Think about your attitude toward taking tests.

As you already know, tests play an important part in determining your final grades in class. Because of this, it is essential that you know not only *how to study* for tests, but also *how to take* tests.

What *do* you know about preparing for and taking tests? Experts report that you have command of only 20 percent of the material when you cram the night before an exam, and that you will probably experience fatigue, loss of concentration, and test anxiety when you study that way. Do you cram or do you review briefly for several nights prior to the test?

Perhaps your difficulty is not with studying for the test, but with taking it. You become so nervous that you find it hard to concentrate on what you know. In this unit you'll find a list of simple techniques to help you eliminate test anxiety.

Once you study your notes and text and conquer your nervousness, all you have to do is sit down with the test and begin answering the questions, right? Not exactly. When you take a test, you show your instructor how much you know about the subject covered, of course. But you *also* show your instructor what you know about test-taking procedures. You may be surprised to learn that there are specific strategies for taking specific kinds of tests; for example, multiple-choice requires a different strategy from true–false.

Do you want to improve your test scores? Study carefully the information in this unit regarding preparing for tests, reducing test-taking anxiety, and taking tests. Your efforts here will earn you better test scores.

Activity 4–1
Memory

To learn how to study for tests, you need to learn the basic principles concerning how your memory works and why you cannot always remember material. It is frustrating to study for several hours the night before a test, only to find you don't remember several important things—even though you can sometimes remember the page they were on. Or, worse yet, you manage to remember those elusive things just as you hand in the test and leave the room.

There is a simple explanation for this, and it has to do with how your memory works. Start a section of notes entitled "Test Taking." Then read the selection entitled "How Your Memory Works." As you read, write down what goes on in each layer of memory.

How Your Memory Works

Test! Mention the word, and some people instantly feel fearful and tense. Yet, if you take time to prepare ahead for tests, you don't have to experience such stress.

In order to understand how to prepare for tests, it is helpful to know *how* you remember things. In *How to Study in High School,* Jean Snider describes the four memory layers in your brain.

Layer One
Layer One is for short-term memory. If a teacher gives you a definition and you can repeat it immediately, Layer One is at work. But if you are asked to give that definition the next day, chances are very good that you won't be able to remember it. Short-term memory is exactly that; it is useful for many daily, routine things such as making telephone calls or following directions immediately after they are given, but it is *not* useful for passing tests.

Layer Two
Layer Two is for slightly longer retention, Snider says. If your instructor announces a test will be given four days from now, and he or she repeats the announcement several times, the message goes from Layer One to Layer Two of memory. It is the *repetition of the information* that forces it from Layer One to Layer Two, yet Layer Two is still not very reliable. You will study the test material the night before the test. But during the test, some—if not many—of the answers will escape you.

When you spend the night before a test cramming and then can't remember the answers for the test—even though you can picture the page they were on—the explanation for your memory lapse is simple. The information you studied only went as far as Layer Two.

Layer Three

Layer Three offers good retention, providing you *repeat the information several times* and *write it down.* Your writing creates a visual image for your mind to remember.

Say, for example, your instructor provides you with terms and their definitions and you repeat them to yourself several times and write them down. You will have forced that information into Layer Three, and you should expect fairly good recall for the test.

Now you know why it is necessary to take notes on material you need to remember, why a written sample test that you construct prior to the real test is valuable, and why writing down key words as you review is beneficial. Your muscles help you remember as you write, and your memory sees the material on paper again and takes a picture of it.

Layer Four

Snider says the passage of time is a must for forcing material into the fourth layer of memory. You must *repeat* those definitions each night *over a period of time* and *write them down* in order for material to reach Layer Four. But once there, the material is locked in long-term storage.

Smart test takers start reviewing for a test at least three or four days before it will be given. Cramming the night before is not reliable learning. It won't give you the results you want.

Summary

Layer One: no repetition—short-term, unreliable memory.

Layer Two: some repetition—slightly longer retention, but not reliable.

Layer Three: repeating and writing down the information—fairly good retention.

Layer Four: repeating and writing down information over a period of three to six days—excellent retention.*

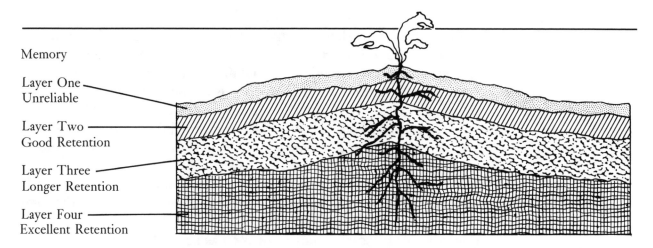

Memory

Layer One
Unreliable

Layer Two
Good Retention

Layer Three
Longer Retention

Layer Four
Excellent Retention

*Snider, Jean. *How to Study in High School.* Providence, RI: Jamestown Publishers, 1983, pp. 36–38.

Activity 4–2
How Do You Prepare for Tests?

Now that you know how your memory works, find out how you can organize your study time to suit your memory. In preparing for a test, do you reread the chapter the night before the test? Perhaps you review your notes or answer the questions at the end of the chapter. Have you ever tried to create a sample test for yourself or have someone quiz you?

Using a separate sheet of paper, make a list of the steps you take in preparing for an exam. List everything you do and when you do it. Then, if your instructor allows time, compare your list with your classmates' lists. Brainstorm as many different ways to prepare for tests as you can, and write down each of the methods on your sheet of paper.

If you are doing this exercise as an independent study, interview five successful students you know to find out how they prepare for exams. Or, interview five different instructors for their ideas on studying for tests. Whichever method you choose, be sure to include the results of your interviews in your notes. You will be sharing these results with your instructor.

Activity 4–3
How Should You Prepare for Tests?

You know how you prepare for tests, and now you know how your classmates go about it. How do your methods compare? Think about some of the new ideas or techniques for preparation that you learned from your peers. Based on what you know about their methods, can you see why one student scores well on tests, while another scores poorly?

The exercise should make this much clear: Rereading the entire chapter the night before a test is a waste of time. Your memory can't possibly absorb and retain all that material in one night. Instead, anticipate questions you think will be asked and review their answers three to six days in advance of the test date.

Now, compare your list of preparation techniques with the list that follows; add any suggestions your list did not include. When you finish, you will have a list of study techniques that, if you use them, will enable you to do well on *any* exam.

Preparing for Tests

1. Ask or anticipate *what material* will be covered on the test and write it down. You can do this by doing the following:

   Look at tests from other chapters and ask your instructor, or students who have taken the class before, what material might be included.

Listen to verbal clues in class. (Verbal clues are like signal words; they "flag" what your instructor considers to be important and may include on the test. Verbal clues are phrases such as "Be sure to remember that . . ."; "Take notes on this . . ."; "You may see this again . . . .")

Pay attention to what your instructor writes on the chalkboard. Write it in your notes and use your highlighter pen to emphasize it; there is a good chance questions relating to it will be on the test.

2. Find out what *type of questions* will be on the test.

Use a different study technique for an essay test than for an objective test. Solving problems involves different preparation than sentence completion does.

Look at past tests to discover your instructor's usual test format.

Ask your instructor, or students who have had the class before, what types of questions will be included.

Listen to lectures and class discussions for clues about the kinds of questions that might be included.

Pay attention to the kinds of exercises you do daily in class; the test may parallel these.

3. Discover how much of the test is based on your notes.

Consider your instructor's attitude about note taking—required or optional. It's a clue to whether he or she will test over notes.

Talk to students who have had the class before, or ask your instructor if you will be tested over the notes.

Analyze previous tests to determine the extent of test material drawn from notes.

4. Organize your notes and other study aids to correspond with the material you believe will be covered and the type of test to be given.

Gather the material you feel might be on the test (notes, chapter review, problems, etc.).

Highlight in your notes the key points that might be covered.

Use margin notes (key words written in the margin) to identify main points.

Write down any additional information you anticipate will be covered.

5. Avoid cramming. Keep in mind that it takes time to get material into the third and fourth layers of your memory, so begin reviewing the material three to six days prior to the test:

First night—skim the material.

Second night—skim the material, read margin notes, and recite important points aloud as you read them. (Those of you who learn best by hearing things should study that way, too. Hear yourself *say* the key points to be learned.)

Third night—read your margin notes (key words) and, without looking at your notes or the text, recite aloud the important points they represent.

Fourth night—make up a sample test and answer the questions, or have someone quiz you. If you do well, you do not need to study a fifth night. If you feel you need to do better, look over the material again and repeat this process a fifth, and perhaps a sixth, night.

6. Prepare yourself the night before the test.

Briefly review the material one more time (if you are a night person and do your best work at night).

Get adequate sleep.

7. Prepare yourself the next day.

Briefly review the material one more time when you wake up (if you are a morning person and do your best work during the morning).

Eat a nutritious breakfast (not donuts and coffee).

Get your mind and body stimulated with brief exercise (short jog, walk, push-ups) and a shower.

Wear something comfortable that makes you feel confident.

Get rid of test anxiety (see Activity 4–4).

Avoid drugs (drugs make you feel sluggish or nervous and affect your ability to recall and concentrate).

Build your self-confidence (tell yourself you have prepared well and so you will do well; a good attitude yields good results).

Exercise is a great way to reduce test anxiety.

Activity 4–4
Test Anxiety

There are just a few minutes to wait before your instructor puts a test in front of you. Are you feeling fidgety and tense, or even sick to your stomach?

If that describes how you feel before you take a test, you probably have test anxiety. Test anxiety is common for most everyone; even the best students have it. But, if you are to do well on a test, your test anxiety must be controlled. How can you control it? Practice some of the following tips.

Read the suggestions below and, on a separate sheet of paper, write down the tips you feel will be valuable for you. Not all of these suggestions work for everyone because people have different personalities. For some, thumbing through the book prior to an exam builds confidence and reassures them that they know the material. For others, it creates panic because they are afraid they may have forgotten to study something. Those people are better off leaving their textbooks at home. Consider each suggestion, then write down only those that will work for you.

Relieving Test Anxiety

1. Get enough sleep.

2. Eat a good meal prior to the test.

    Do not eat too much so that you feel groggy, but eat enough to provide your mind and body with the calories they need to function well.

    Greasy and acidic food and beverages (donuts and coffee) will not provide adequate nutrition and may upset your stomach.

3. Exercise to reduce tension and stimulate thinking.

   Exercise is a great stress reducer. Jogging, walking, mild aerobics, push-ups, and other forms of exercise will not only reduce test anxiety, but will stimulate your mind and body to improve your ability to think and concentrate as well.

4. Take a shower.

   Warm water relaxes some; cold water stimulates others.

5. Allow enough time to arrive at the class without hurrying.

   Hurrying causes tension; the fear of being late builds anxiety.

6. Provide yourself with time in the classroom to relax and compose yourself.

   Deep breathing exercises accomplish this. Take a deep breath, then another short breath, and exhale slowly.

   Close your eyes and imagine a relaxing scene. Allow your muscles to relax. Then think about your test while you are in this relaxed state.

7. Review with your friends *or* Don't review with your friends just prior to the test.

   For some, reviewing with friends before the exam builds confidence; it causes them to feel they have command of the material. For others, it incites panic; it makes them feel they don't know the material as well as they should.

8. Thumb through your books and notes *or* Don't thumb through your books and notes just prior to the test.

   Thumb through your notes if it builds confidence; don't look at your notes if doing so creates panic.

9. Develop a positive attitude.

   Tell yourself you studied as well as you could have for the test and *believe it*. Convince yourself that others have done well on this test, and you can, too.

10. Make sure you can see a clock, plan your time, and pace yourself.

    Not knowing how much of the test-taking time has elapsed creates anxiety. Budget your time, so you have time to answer all of the questions.

11. Choose your seat carefully.

    Sitting near friends can be disrupting. If you see them writing furiously, it can make you nervous. If you see them handing in their papers early, you may feel compelled to do the same, and your anxiety will build.

    Some people may read the test questions softly but audibly as they concentrate. Others may chew gum loudly. These are distractions that may annoy you and cause anxiety. Isolate yourself, if possible.

12. Begin by filling in the answers you know.

    This builds confidence and relieves anxiety because you see that you *do* know the answers. Also, it may trigger recall of other answers that you had momentarily forgotten.

13. Don't panic if others are busy writing and you are not.

    By spending time thinking, you may provide higher quality and better content answers than someone who is writing frantically.

14. Don't panic if you forget an answer.

    Go on to other questions—the answer will probably occur to you as you continue taking the test.

15. Don't worry if others finish before you do.

    Finishing first does not guarantee the best grade. Usually the better papers are handed in by the students who spent more time thinking about and checking over their answers before turning in their papers.

16. Don't panic if you run out of time.

    Ask your instructors if you can stay late; many will let you do this to finish.

Outline essay questions you didn't have time to complete. Most instructors will give some points for outlines because they can see you knew the answers, but didn't have time to write them in essay form.

Activity 4–5
Strategies for Taking Tests

Now that you know how to handle the pretest jitters, you need to consider what to do when that test is in your hands. If you are a person who gulps and says "Go for it," you are probably not getting the highest grades you could get. Instead, try using a few test-taking strategies.

The first one is simple: Read the directions on the test carefully *before* you begin writing. If you miss the words "Choose one of the following three essay questions," and you try to answer all three questions, you'll probably run out of time and give incomplete answers. There are fewer unpleasant surprises when you read the directions.

Perhaps you have been in this unfortunate situation: You are running out of test-taking time, and you still have to complete two essay questions. For the first time, you notice that they are worth twenty points each, and now you don't have enough time to give thorough answers.

Who needs to use test-taking strategies? We all do. Remember, you are not only being tested on the material, you are also being tested on how much you know about taking a test. So, to do the best you can on tests, you have to think about your own test-taking strategies. On a separate sheet of paper, list the steps or strategies you use when taking a test. After you finish, compare your list with your classmates' and, working as a class, develop a more comprehensive list. (If you are in an independent study, interview five successful students to compare your list with their lists of test-taking strategies, adding any new ones to your list.)

Now, compare your comprehensive list of test-taking strategies with the one below, and add to your list any techniques that you had not previously included.

Test-taking strategies help with tests on any subject.

Test-taking Strategies

1. Arrive early.

   Allow enough time to compose your thoughts, sharpen your concentration, organize your materials, and relax.

2. Bring all materials to class with you.

   Bring pencils or pens, paper, erasers, calculator (and extra batteries), and any other materials necessary for taking that test.

3. Listen carefully to your instructor's directions and comments.

   Instructors frequently announce changes in the test or emphasize instructions you may overlook; pay attention to what they have to say.

4. Look over the test, reading the directions carefully.

   If you don't answer the questions as instructed, you may lose points. Even an instruction as simple as "Write the complete word *true*" can cost you points if you don't follow it.

5. Budget your time.

   You should spend less time on a five-point completion than you spend on a twenty-point essay question.

   Determine the amount of time you have to take the test and the value and difficulty of each section. Then budget your time accordingly.

   If you have twenty questions and sixty minutes, spend three minutes per question; if you have four questions, each worth twenty-five points, and sixty minutes, spend fifteen minutes on each question.

   If you don't complete a question in the time you allotted, leave it and come back to complete your answer *only* if you have extra time.

6. Write down key facts or formulas in the margin.

   This is a safeguard against forgetting key information if you get nervous.

7. Look for qualifying words.

   Words such as *never, always, rarely, often, seldom, many,* and so on determine the correct answer.

8. Answer easy questions first.

   Answering the easy questions first will reduce anxiety, build confidence, trigger recall of other answers and the material you studied, and give you points immediately. You will be able to say to yourself, "This isn't so bad after all; I'm going to do well." And you'll approach the test with more vigor and confidence. Tackling the tough questions first may make you feel unprepared and uninformed, setting you up for failure.

9. Answer objective questions before essay questions.

   Completing the true–false, multiple-choice, and matching questions may provide you with answers to the essay questions.

10. If you don't know the answer, make a mark next to that question and try to complete it later.

    Often, answers you can't recall will occur to you as you take the test. If you have provided your memory with enough information, you will think of the answer. If not, don't panic—even the best students face this situation. Neatly write down the most suitable answer you can think of, and continue.

11. Guess at answers you don't know, unless there is a penalty for guessing.

    On true–false questions, you have a 50 percent chance of guessing right; on multiple-choice questions, you often have a 25 percent chance of being correct. Don't pass up potential points by leaving the question blank.

The only time you are penalized for guessing is when, in scoring the results, the number wrong is to be subtracted from the number correct. Not very many instructors use this technique, however. Most subtract the number wrong from the total possible.

12. Change answers *only* if you are sure they are wrong.

Most sources say first instincts are usually correct; however, sometimes you will recall information that will lead you to believe your first answer was incorrect. If so, make the change.

13. Use all the time allowed.

If you finish early, check your paper for errors.

Look again at the directions; did you follow them correctly?

Activity 4–6
Tricks for Taking Tests

Now you know that there are definite techniques for taking tests, and you have learned the best way to approach tests in general. You are ready for some details. There are specific tricks you can use to take a true–false test, or a multiple-choice test, or an essay test, for example. If you don't know these tricks, you are at a definite disadvantage, and your grades will reflect it.

To your notes on test taking, add a page labeled "Tricks for Taking Tests." List the following types of tests and, beneath each, write any tricks you already use when taking that kind of test. Leave plenty of space to add additional tricks in each section. The types of tests include: True–False, Multiple-Choice, Matching, Completion, and Essay.

Compare your list of tricks with those of your classmates, add to your list, and then compare your comprehensive list with the one that follows. If you are in an independent study, go directly to the following list and fill in the tricks you are missing.

Tests-taking Tricks

True–False
1. Beware of qualifying words.

Words such as *always, all, none, never,* and so on **usually** will make a statement false. Very few facts are absolute, and one exception to such a question will make it false.

Words such as *usually, sometimes, generally,* and *frequently* will **usually** make a statement true.

2. Look at the length of the statement.

   In order for a statement to be true, all parts of it must be true. The longer the statement, the more room there is for a false segment.

3. Be aware of false logic.

   Two statements that are true may be linked with a word that makes them false. Watch for that connecting word. For example: "The U.S. space shuttle program is famous because there was a shuttle crash." The shuttle program **is** famous and there **was** a shuttle crash, but the crash is not what made the program famous. The *because* makes the statement false.

4. Guess if you don't know the answer.

   You have a 50 percent chance of answering correctly, so take the chance.

Multiple-Choice

1. Eliminate the answer(s) that is (are) obviously incorrect first.

   Instructors usually structure a multiple-choice question with one statement that is obviously incorrect. Pick out that statement.

2. Read the question carefully.

   The question may say "Which is *not* an example of . . . ," "Which is the *incorrect* answer . . . ," or "Choose the *best* answer . . . ."

3. Read all the choices.

   You may believe that the first option is the correct one. Read the remaining options anyway. The most correct answer may be further down the list.

4. Pay attention to "all of the above" questions.

   "All of the above" is frequently the correct answer when it appears as a choice. To determine the extent of students' knowl-

edge, instructors occasionally like to list several correct answers and conclude with "all of the above."

If two statements appear to be true, you are unsure about the third statement, and the fourth choice is "all of the above," the fourth choice is often correct.

5. Look for the longest answer.

The longest multiple-choice answer is frequently the correct one. The answer is carefully constructed to be complete.

Matching

1. Read the list on the right first.

First, read the list on the right, which contains the answer choices, so that you are aware of all the possibilities for answers.

Your instructor may have written one answer that appears to be correct near the top of the list, but a more correct answer may come lower in the list. If you do not read the entire list first, you will not know all the options.

2. If you are unsure of an answer, mark that question and return to it later.

Solve these by process of elimination after you have finished using the answers you are sure are correct.

Completion (Fill-in-the-Blank)

1. Reread the question several times.

Completion is popular with instructors because they can simply write down a statement and leave out a key word(s).

In rereading the question several times, the key word(s) omitted may, because of the repetition, suddenly occur to you.

2. Look for context clues.

Often, within a completion there are clues to the correct answer. If the blank you are to complete is at the end of the statement,

you have more clues to use than if the blank falls at the beginning of the statement.

3. *A* and *an* are context clues.

   If *an* appears, the word following must begin with a vowel.

4. Look at the verb in the sentence.

   If it is singular, the subject or answer must be singular. If it is plural, the subject or answer must be plural.

5. Mark the statements you cannot complete and return to them.

   Recall of the information you need may be triggered by completing other statements.

Essay

1. Plan your time carefully.

   It is easy to lose track of time when writing an essay question response; budget your time and stick to your budget.

2. Know your facts.

   In objective tests, such as multiple-choice and matching, you have to select the correct answer from other choices given. In answering essay questions, you must frame your own answer, and to do it correctly, you must know the information needed.

3. Organize or outline your answers.

   In the margin, on the back of the paper, or in the space for the answer, write an outline first. List the facts and number them according to the order in which you wish to discuss them.

   Outlines enable you to present all the key information in an abbreviated, organized manner. You are less likely to omit important information or ramble in your answer if you outline first.

   If you have the key information in an outline, but run out of time in writing your essay, most instructors will give you partial credit for the outline. They can see you knew the information.

Answers presented in a helter-skelter fashion do not represent the logic, reasoning, and organization instructors look for in an essay answer. If your essay is not organized, you will probably lose points.

4. Understand the test terminology.

Be certain that you understand what is being asked when the essay question instructs you to compare and/or contrast. *Evaluate* is different from *analyze* and *interpret* is different from *illustrate*. Activity 4–7 will give you some practice in reviewing these terms.

5. Write neatly, leave suitable margins, and provide space between answers.

A good answer is not good at all if it is illegible. Most instructors penalize for sloppy work and look more favorably on work that is neatly done.

6. Write using complete sentences.

Essays require complete sentences. Hurried thoughts scribbled in brief do not comply with the more formal essay structure.

7. Restate the question in the first sentence of your essay.

Don't stumble around. Get right to the point. If the question is "Discuss the seven ways to improve your study setting," your answer should begin with "The first of the seven ways to improve my study setting involves . . . ."

Your instructor will know you are going to be concise and logical and will begin with a favorable attitude toward your answer.

8. Use transition words to emphasize your organization.

Tie your thoughts and concepts together with transitions such as the following: *for example, because, for this reason, however, likewise, in summary, ultimately*. There are many transition words you can choose.

9. Keep your answer simple and concise.

Avoid flowery language that is meant to pad an answer with words but no information. Instructors can see through that.

10. Identify the favorite concepts of your instructor and use them.

   If your instructor is sure that TV has ruined the study habits of millions of students, and he or she seems to dwell on that concept, use it in your discussion if it applies.

11. Include a conclusion or summary.

   Restate your major points in your summary or conclusion. This step will reassure your instructor of your logic, organization, and key points.

Activity 4–7
Test Terminology

One of the main points mentioned previously involved knowing what type of answer was being asked for on an essay test. *Trace, discuss, justify, review, illustrate*—are you familiar with the subtle differences in test terminology? You can write a lengthy essay answer full of facts and logic, but if you did not address the question, you may score no points at all.

Consider the following terms typically found in essay exams. On a separate sheet of paper, list each term and an explanation of what is required when answering that type of essay question. If you don't know or are not sure what the term means, leave the space next to the term blank and fill in the correct answer later.

A. list	E. summarize	I. compare
B. outline	F. trace	J. contrast
C. define	G. describe	K. discuss
D. criticize	H. diagram	L. justify

How did you do? Sometimes just knowing what answers are suitable for particular terms found on essay tests can add points to your total score. Compare your list of terms and definitions with those found at the end of this unit in the Appendix. Correct any errors you made and add those answers you omitted. This list of terms should be added to your section of notes on Test Taking.

Activity 4–8
Reviewing Your Test

Let's assume you have prepared properly for an upcoming test, reduced the test anxiety successfully, followed the strategies you learned for taking tests, and applied the tricks for taking specific kinds of tests. Now you have the completed, corrected test in your hands.

Do you trash it? File it? Frame it? You should analyze it—not by quickly glancing through it, but by spending time studying it. To complete this unit on test taking successfully, you need to analyze the completed, corrected product and use the information to prepare for future exams.

What kind of questions did your instructor include?

What material did your instructor cover—textbook, lecture notes, exercises from class, or some combination?

What was your instructor looking for in your answers?

What were your strengths in answering the questions?

What were your weak areas?

What test-taking strategies do you need to use again next time?

What changes do you need to make?

Use a test that you have taken recently, either from this class or another, and analyze it. On a separate sheet of paper, using the test you have supplied, answer the questions from the list preceding this paragraph.

Analyzing a corrected test is an excellent way to discover your test-taking strengths and weaknesses.

Activity 4–9
Unit Review

On a separate sheet of paper, answer the following questions. Try to remember the main points and tips given in Unit 4.

I. True–False
    Number from one to twenty. Write *true* if the statement is true and *false* if the statement is false.

1. When studying, repetition (repeating things several times) is not necessary for remembering things.

2. The passing of time is necessary for forcing material into your memory so that you can remember it for a long period of time.

3. You must repeat material several times *and* write it down in order to remember things well; it is not enough to simply repeat it.

4. It takes approximately three to six nights prior to an essay test for proper review of the material.

5. It takes only one night prior to an objective test for proper review of the material since objective tests are somewhat easier.

6. It is always enough preparation when studying for a test to review your notes and go over chapter headings.

7. Wearing something that makes them feel comfortable and confident helps some people do better on exams.

8. It is helpful when beginning a test to write down important facts or a formula you might otherwise forget as you take the test.

9. Answer the easy questions last and tackle the hard questions first. They are usually worth more points and you need to be sure you complete them.

10. Answer the essay questions before the objective questions. They are usually worth more points and you need to be sure you complete them.

11. When answering essay questions, outline your responses first, but do not write the outline down on your test paper.

12. Before beginning a test, budget your time. You should spend about the same amount of time on each question.

13. On true–false questions, you should generally choose the answer that was your first instinct. It is usually correct.

14. On multiple-choice tests you can usually eliminate one answer as being incorrect.

15. When taking a matching test, read the left-hand column first and then choose the correct answer from the right-hand column.

16. You should not guess on fill-in-the-blank questions.

17. You can reduce test-taking stress by doing deep-breathing exercises.

18. Some people reduce test-taking stress by thumbing through their textbooks just prior to exam time.

19. For many people, coffee and a donut are all they need for breakfast, even on the morning of a test day.

20. Exercise not only reduces stress, it also stimulates thinking.

II. Matching
Number from twenty-one to thirty. Match the following descriptions with the test terminologies they describe.

21. Give differences only.

22. Give meanings but no details.

23. Give details, progress, or history from beginning to end.

24. Prove or give reasons.

25. Provide a numbered list.

26. Give details or a verbal picture.

27. Give reasons pro and con with details.

28. Give both similarities and differences.

29. Give a series of main ideas supported by secondary ideas.

30. Give your own judgment or opinion based on reasons.

A. list

B. outline

C. define

D. criticize

E. trace

F. describe

G. compare

H. contrast

I. discuss

J. justify

K. summarize

III. Listing
Number from thirty-one to thirty-seven, and list seven steps in preparing for a test.

IV. Essay
Choose *one* of the following essay questions and answer it using the essay format discussed in Unit 4.

A. Discuss test anxiety. Begin by defining it and then describe ways that you can control it. (First identify controls that work for you, and then identify additional controls that may work for someone else.)

B. Describe the steps in taking a test. Include as many steps as you can.

C. Discuss the four layers of memory. Include the function of each layer, how you get information into that layer, and which layer you should use for test-taking preparation.

Appendix
Answers for Activity 4–7

Test Terminology

Term	*Answer Would Include:*
A. list	a numbered list of words, sentences, or comments
B. outline	a series of main ideas supported by secondary ideas, etc.
C. define	meanings but no details; this is often a matter of giving a memorized definition
D. criticize	your own judgment or opinion based on reasons; good and bad points should be included
E. summarize	a brief, condensed account of the main ideas; omit details
F. trace	details, progress, or history of the topic from beginning to end
G. describe	details or a verbal picture of the topic
H. diagram	a chart, graph, or geometric drawing with labels and a brief explanation, if needed
I. compare	both the similarities and the differences
J. contrast	the differences only
K. discuss	reasons pro and con with details
L. justify	prove or give reasons

Improving Your Understanding

IMPROVING (im-prōōv'ing) v. to make or become better

UNDERSTANDING (un-dər-stand'ing) n. the quality of comprehension

ou have just closed your book after reading an entire assignment with what you thought was understanding. But already your mind is blank, and you can't remember anything about what you read. Now you will have to spend more time to reread the paragraph or, worse still, the chapter.

If this situation is all too familiar, you'll be glad to hear that you can improve your comprehension. There are strategies to give you some "mental hooks" on which to hang the information that is vital to your success in school and in life. Learning these comprehension survival skills will take effort, practice, and determination, but you cannot overlook them if you want to be a successful student.

To begin improving comprehension, first learn how to recognize main ideas. If you can identify the main ideas—and remember them—in the material you read, you have almost won the comprehension battle.

Finding the main idea may be difficult for two reasons: First, you may not know what a main idea is. The main idea is simply *the point the author is trying to get across*. It is the gist or substance of a paragraph; the thought that all the other details or pieces of information help to support or illustrate. Ask yourself as you read, "What point is the author making in this paragraph?" The answer to your question is the author's main idea.

The second reason recognizing the main idea may be difficult is that you don't know where in the material to look for it. Is it in the first or last sentence, or is it sandwiched somewhere in the middle of the paragraph? Authors can place their paragraph's main idea anywhere. Look for it to come in the first sentence, a middle sentence, or the last sentence. Or, find it in the first sentence and see it restated in the last sentence, in a middle sentence, or not stated at all! Think of finding the material's main idea as participating in a scavenger hunt; you know what kind of thing to look for, but not exactly where to find it. You'll have to actively search for it.

This unit will help you develop your ability to recognize main ideas. You will begin by selecting the key words in a sentence, then move on to identifying the main idea in a paragraph. Once you can do that, you will practice recognizing main ideas in longer works. Your goals, then, are:

To learn to identify key words in a sentence;

To learn to identify the main idea in a paragraph; and

To learn to identify the major points of a longer selection.

Activity 5–1
Recognizing Key Words in a Sentence

To find the main idea in a paragraph, you have to begin by recognizing key words in a sentence. *Key words* are the *important or essential words*—the words that determine the meaning of the sentence. Activity 5–1 will give you practice in picking out key words.

On a separate sheet of paper, number from one to ten, skipping every other line. Read the following sentences and list their key words on your paper. The first sentence is done as a sample.

1. You are to report to the principal's office immediately and take your books with you.
Answer: You report principal's office immediately take books

2. The tryouts for the fall play will be this Thursday evening at 8:00 P.M. in Room 208.

3. The flood destroyed homes, bridges, and roads as it swept furiously through the canyon.

4. The Fourth of July is a special day in the United States because on that date the nation celebrates its independence.

5. Many states experience wide temperature changes during the four seasons.

6. Susan Smith and Joan Vickers ran for secretary of their class, and Joan won.

7. The football championship was a tie between North and South High Schools.

8. Peer pressure is often a problem for preteens and teens.

9. Regular attendance in school is important if you want to get good grades.

10. Concentration is required as you read these sentences if you wish to identify the key words.

Activity 5–2
Recognizing Main Ideas in a Paragraph

Once you have developed the ability to identify key words in a sentence, you will find it easier to pick out the main idea in a paragraph. Again, the main idea is the point the author is making; all other sentences in the paragraph work to support or develop this main idea.

On a separate sheet of paper, list the key or main idea in each of the following paragraphs. The first paragraph is done as a sample.

Paragraph One

Young people are faced with many decisions today. They have to choose between drinking or not drinking alcohol. They have to choose between smoking or not smoking. Some of them even choose between chewing tobacco or not chewing tobacco. For many, the decisions are difficult ones.

Answer: Young people are faced with many decisions today.

Paragraph Two

If it is sunny outside, do you feel cheerful? If it is rainy, do you feel depressed? Does the weather affect you? Hot weather makes some people irritable. Others complain that humid weather makes them tired.

Paragraph Three

Most schools are required to offer courses in English, math, science, social studies, and physical education. Schools also offer classes in art, industrial arts, computer science, music, foreign languages, agriculture, business, and auto mechanics. They provide opportunities before, during, and after school for sports, clubs, and other activities. Schools counsel students, reward students, correct students, and even feed students, in addition to educating them. Schools serve a variety of needs.

Paragraph Four

Students have many opportunities to become a part of a group and to acquire a sense of belonging. They can try out for sports teams or become a team manager. They can audition for a play or sing in a choir. They can participate on the speech team or be a member of the chess club. They can join a church group or become a peer counselor. There are many ways to get involved.

Paragraph Five

We began the day by touring the Museum of Natural History. After we had lunch, we visited the Museum of Fine Arts and had snacks on the top floor terrace. Next, we went to the Planetarium and finished with dinner at a fancy downtown restaurant.

Paragraph Six

By now you know several things about the main idea of a paragraph. You know the main idea summarizes or expresses the major point being made in the paragraph. You know the main idea can be found at the beginning of a paragraph, at the end of a paragraph, within a paragraph, or at the beginning *and* end of a paragraph. You know most paragraphs have a main idea that is stated, but you also know that the main idea can be omitted and only inferred. Finally, you know that finding the main idea in the paragraph is one of the first steps toward good comprehension.

Activity 5–3
Recognizing Main Ideas in an Article

Now work with an article that contains many paragraphs. Read "Use of Credit" and write down on a separate sheet of paper what you consider to be the main ideas of the article. As you read, remember to ask yourself the following: What points are the authors making in this selection?

Next, focus on the supporting details in the article. List the advantages and disadvantages of credit.

Use of Credit

Credit is one money management tool. It is considered a tool because it can be used to realize the goals that you have decided to emphasize. Credit can expand buying power and simplify recordkeeping; however, if credit purchases are not related to income and payments are missed, the result is a poor credit history and financial worries. In some cases use of too much credit may lead to bankruptcy.

Credit use can be inexpensive or costly. Many credit grantors do not charge interest for credit card purchases when the balance is paid in full each month. Other types of credit such as consumer loans may add interest charges of 36 percent per year. You can decide which type fits your needs.

Consider both the advantages and disadvantages of using credit. As you think about the ways that credit plays a role in your money management program, you may decide to either expand or reduce your use of credit. Credit decisions are very individual and can have beneficial as well as disastrous consequences. This means that you will have to make a conscious decision about how to use credit.

Advantages

Young people often have greater needs than current income. Credit may be the way to make large purchases such as a home, education, furniture, and appliances.

By borrowing to buy an item, people will have the use of it before they own it. A good example is an automobile—few people can afford to pay cash, and yet this is considered an essential purchase for most people.

Sometimes the only way to cope with an emergency is to borrow to pay expenses, especially when emergency medical care is needed or unemployment reduces income.

Credit can be used for investments. A house is important for shelter and in recent years has been an excellent investment. Most people usually do not have cash to buy a home.

Credit allows people to enjoy conveniences today. Some families find washing clothes at home rather than at a laundromat a real time-saver. A loan may provide an opportunity to add a second bathroom to a home with a growing family.

Using a credit card while traveling can be a great convenience over carrying large amounts of money or trying to cash personal checks.

For people who find it difficult to save for purchases, credit payments may be considered a form of forced savings.

There are tax advantages for borrowers. Interest is tax deductible for those who itemize expenses.

Disadvantages

Consumers may overspend. One-third of all U.S. households have bank credit cards and 70 percent of those who use cards generally pay only the minimum monthly payment. We have the tendency to spend more money when we charge items compared to paying cash. Researchers concerned with department store purchases found that the average cash sale was $8.25, the average store credit card purchase was $15.93, and the average bank card sale was $20.47. Many people have more than one bank card. When their line of credit on one card is used up, they switch to another card.

Credit has been relatively easy to get and consumers have found themselves adding credit card to credit card and loan on top of loan to their outstanding debt.

People overlook the fact that when they buy an item they are paying twice for it. First for the item itself and second for the credit they use.

Finance charges add to the price of goods and services. For example, we'll assume that a loan is for a travel trailer. The cost of the trailer is $5,000. The credit charges add an additional $902.32 to the price. Credit ties up future income which means less flexibility for tomorrow's purchases.

Activity 5–4
Recognizing Sequence by Making Lists

If organization is a strong skill of yours, sequencing (placing things in order) may not seem difficult. If, on the other hand, you often ask yourself "What shall I do first?" or "Why are things so disorganized?" this group of exercises will help you to begin thinking sequentially. Remembering becomes much easier when you can arrange the information you read in some sort of order, and catching on to the sequence will improve your comprehension skills as well. Your goal is to read and place things in your mind and memory in logical order.

Making Lists

Determine a heading for each of the following sentences. On a separate sheet of paper, write the heading and list the items in the sentence sequentially as they are presented. The first is done for you.

1. My grocery list included apples, flour, salt, and sugar.
   Answer: Groceries

      1. apples
      2. flour
      3. salt
      4. sugar

2. As he entered the room, he stopped with mouth wide open and eyes rounded in horror.

3. Mr. Smith presented two band awards this year: the Spirit Award and the prestigious John Phillip Sousa Award.

4. The following local scholarships are available to seniors: Columbine Honor Society, Elks, Altrusa, Frank-McKee Memorial, Lions' Club, Music Teachers, and Rotary Club International.

5. As she looked forward to a new school year, Sue knew she would need to purchase a backpack, pens, pencils, paper, spiral notebooks, an eraser, and a highlighter.

Activity 5–5
Recognizing Sequence by Putting Steps in Order

Determining the order in which to do things requires comprehension or understanding. Try your hand at the following passage in which the steps are scrambled. Unscramble the steps and write them in the logical order on your paper.

How to Scramble Eggs

Pour in mixture and reduce heat to low. Heat ½ tablespoon fat for each egg in moderately hot skillet. Break eggs into bowl. When cooked through but still moist (5 to 8 minutes), serve at once. Add 1 tablespoon milk or cream and a dash of salt and pepper for each egg. Cook slowly, turning gently as mixture sets at bottom and sides of pan. Beat well with a fork. Avoid constant stirring.

Activity 5–6
Recognizing Sequence by Listing Procedures

Now try your skills on a longer selection. This time you will sequence procedures. Read the questions below, so you know your purpose for reading the selection and the questions you should be answering as you read. Then read the selection. On a separate sheet of paper:

1. List the three time periods involved in a job interview. Leave space below each time period.

2. Under each time period, list the important points or tips for that portion of the interview.

Conclude by writing a brief paragraph summarizing the sequence of procedures in a job interview.

Be sure to dress appropriately for an interview. Different clothes are right for different jobs.

The Job Interview

Once you have an appointment for a job interview, there are certain things that should be done. These can basically be divided into three time periods—before, during, and after the interview.

Dress appropriately as you prepare for the interview. Wear clothes that are commonly worn or accepted in your interviewer's profession. If you're not sure what is appropriate to wear, ask for advice from others, or someone you know in that profession. Dress as if you could go to work at that location immediately.

Go to the interview alone and arrive five to ten minutes early. Being early shows that you are eager and responsible enough to be prompt. You must have done your homework, of course, and know what the company you hope to join makes or the services it provides.

Before leaving for the interview, be sure that you have your Social Security card, several copies of your résumé, and the names, addresses, and phone numbers of at least three people who are not relatives to be used as references or sources of information about you. If the job would include driving as part of the duties, take your driver's license, as well.

During the interview, be polite. Don't smoke or chew gum. Try to look as alert as possible, neither slouching nor sitting ramrod straight. Make frequent eye contact and listen intently to what the interviewer is

saying. Answer his or her questions clearly and completely, speaking audibly. *Do not mumble.* Don't hesitate to ask questions of the interviewer as they occur to you, but wait to ask about benefits and vacations until you are actually offered the job. If you are not offered the job but want it, say so to the interviewer. Do not be demanding; simply state confidently that you would like to have the position.

After the interview, be sure to thank the interviewer for spending his or her time to talk with you. After the interview, write a thank-you note. This is a polite gesture, often neglected, that may help the interviewer to keep you in mind.

If you were told by the interviewer that he or she would contact you, and you do not get a response, call or make a return visit. Perseverance often wins jobs.

Activity 5–7
Understanding Character Development

You probably remember being asked to read a piece of literature and describe its main character. You were to discuss what the person was like at the beginning of the book and how that person changed. This kind of assignment also involves sequencing. Your purpose in reading required you to trace, in an orderly fashion from the beginning to the conclusion, the development of the main character.

Try that with the following paragraphs. On a separate sheet of paper, first list details that describe the new employee at the beginning of the story, then at the middle of the story, and, finally, at the end of the story. Then list, in the order they appeared or happened, the people and events that caused the main character to change.

Experience and a big smile can make a difficult job easier.

At Last—The Job!

I had passed the test of the interview with flying colors, was given *the* job, and had started to work. Before, my experience had come chiefly from TV, movies, and my imagination. Unfortunately, mind games had not prepared me for the difficult period of adjustment that every inexperienced waitress must face: mixed-up orders, tired feet, spilled Coke, irate customers, crying babies, tired feet, littered tables, sticky plates, and tired feet—and all for small tips.

As you can imagine, I soon became so discouraged with myself and so dissatisfied with my job that I was considering quitting. I think my supervisor must have felt the negative vibrations coming from my exhausted self, because she called me into her office and talked to me about both the duties of my new profession and the challenges they presented for sharpening my organizational skills to a fine edge. She also pointed out the direct relationship between my organizational abilities and service and the size of my tip.

That conversation with her helped me to change my attitude considerably. I realized then that there was nothing wrong with me or my job that experience and a big smile could not cure, so I decided to stay on.

Activity 5–8
Visualizing Character

As you improve your comprehension skills, you will gain a broader understanding of what you read. You also will remember more if you can train yourself to project mentally beyond the printed, literal meanings.

Think about the new employee in Activity 5–7. What kind of a visual image do you have of that person? Is that person a young girl or a middle-aged woman? How does she look, dress, and act? Through the course of the story, how does she change? Creating a vivid visual image in your mind of a character helps you to remember the content of what you read.

Try it. As you read, create a visual image of the characters or scenes being presented in the following five descriptions. Draw from your own experiences and observations. Become that person! It's fun, and you will be surprised at how much longer and more vivid your memory of what you read will be.

On a separate sheet of paper, write a description of the character you "see" in each of the sentences below.

1. Long lashes lowered, she scuffed her patent leather shoes in the dust as she pulled at the ribbon that was her sash.

2. Always shabby in dress and committed to saving aluminum cans, he never went out to lunch unless I was buying.

3. Massive in stature, his bellowing voice and swooping gestures, combined with his unkempt grey hair and grizzled beard, tended to put people off.

4. His changes of mood and wide-eyed whoops of laughter made his strange predictions very unsettling.

5. As the model pivoted on the runway, teeth flashing, golden tresses flying, and skirts swirling, I imagined a regal queen, accepting homage from loyal subjects.

Activity 5-9
Understanding Character Through Background

If you read about a character, visualizing and working for an understanding of him or her based on details of the character's life, you have good comprehension of the character as a whole.

As you read the following paragraphs, try to visualize and then understand the great composer Johannes Brahms. Then, on a separate sheet of paper, answer these questions:

1. Why did Brahms never dare to try marriage?

2. Form an opinion or make a judgment regarding Brahms' character; justify your own view of it based on your understanding of the man.

Johannes Brahms, 1833–1897

Few great composers had more difficult early years than Brahms. When Brahms was in his teens, he would perform in the waterfront saloons to earn money for his family. Even then, Brahms never used sheet music, for he could play everything from memory.

When he was twenty, Brahms was introduced by letter to the noted composer Robert Schumann. Schumann and his wife, Clara, took Brahms and his music to their hearts. When it became necessary for Schumann to enter an asylum for the insane, Brahms comforted Clara and gradually fell in love with her. Even after Schumann died, two years later, Brahms never spoke of marriage. (He was known for becoming very close to several women, only to bow out of the relationship.) Brahms once said that there were two things he had never dared to try: opera and marriage.

Brahms spent the last half of his life in Vienna, a noted city of music. He was seen as a privately generous, publicly crusty, boorish bachelor. He lived in the simplest of rooms and rose every morning at five o'clock. With his baggy, unimpressive appearance, bulky form, high voice, and his shovel-shaped beard, he was a familiar figure. Those that knew him loved that part of him which was forever young.

This rather disheveled, outwardly eccentric man, who kept his money tied up in bundles and got some of his best ideas while shining his shoes, was one of the supreme architects of complex, orderly musical structure—the symphony.

Activity 5–10
Sensing Relationships Between Cause and Effect

As your comprehension skills grow sharper, you will soon realize that many of your classes deal, very basically, with what happened first and second and then third to cause an end result. Think of studying the Civil War, for example. You begin by looking at the causes of the war, then the war itself, and finally the effects of the war on the United States and even the world.

Sometimes events are not clearly spelled out in a simple first-second-third sequence, however, and you must dig to uncover information. If you have to make a search, it is helpful to first clearly identify what happened (the cause). Then use your skills at locating key thoughts and proper sequence to uncover the clues necessary to find the target result (or the effect).

Practice identifying reading clues and targets, and your comprehension skills will improve even more because you are alert as you read, actively searching for answers. Your reading rate will improve because you know exactly what you are looking for.

Consider the following example. Jerry has gotten a poor grade on a test because he didn't study, but instead of accepting the grade, he begins arguing with his instructor in an attempt to get more points. After several unsuccessful attempts on Jerry's part, the instructor firmly responds, "Jerry, that's enough!" Jerry is silent.

By following the sequence and reading between the lines, what does this example say to you? The content reveals exactly what Jerry has done and how his instructor responded. But beyond that, what else do you know?

Jerry was silent. What did Jerry anticipate?

What can you point to as the cause of the instructor's response?

How would you describe the instructor's mood?

What would you anticipate would happen if Jerry continued to argue?

You can see that the answers to these questions are not printed in the paragraph above. To come up with the answers, you have to think beyond what is printed. And to do that, you use higher-level thinking skills.

Concentrate on the sequence of events as you read the following paragraphs. After you finish reading, consider the relationships that are established between the "causes" and the "effects" to answer the questions that follow each paragraph. Write your answers on a separate sheet of paper.

Paragraph One

It is a beautiful, sunny summer day, and Tony and Roberto decide to go fishing. Tony grabs the fishing poles and a net, Roberto packs a quick lunch, and they set off. When they reach the lake, they discover they are missing an important item for their fishing excursion.

1. What are Tony and Roberto missing?

2. What will be the effect of fishing without this item?

3. Conversely, if they catch no fish, what is the cause?

Paragraph Two

Yoshimi has gone to the store to buy a birthday present for her mother. She has ten dollars that her father gave her along with specific instructions as to what to purchase. She is to buy a necklace her mother has been hinting about for weeks. As she passes by the store window, Yoshimi sees a purse that she just *has to* have. The purse is on sale for five dollars, and she buys it. She buys her mother a small pair of earrings with the remaining money.

1. What will Yoshimi's father's reaction be?

2. What is the cause of his reaction?

3. What will Yoshimi's mother's reaction be?

4. What is the cause of her reaction?

5. How will her parents' reactions affect Yoshimi?

Paragraph Three

Sean has a part-time job after school at a small grocery store. It is his responsibility to gather the grocery carts from the parking lot and bring them indoors. After the first month of work, he arrives on Tuesday twenty minutes late; his boss comments on it. The following Tuesday he arrives twenty minutes late again; his boss warns him about being late. Again, the next Tuesday, Sean arrives twenty minutes late. His boss is in the parking lot gathering the grocery carts himself.

1. What do you anticipate Sean's boss will do?

2. What are the causes of his boss's actions?

3. Is this "result" fair for Sean?

Activity 5–11
Analyzing Causes and Their Effects

Sometimes, causes and their effects are not obvious as you read. To understand the material, you may need to *analyze* it. For example, if you fail a test, you need to analyze the causes of your failing in order to avoid failing again. Once you determine why your test answers were incorrect, you can avoid repeating the same kinds of mistakes on a second test. You analyze the cause of making mistakes to avoid their effect—failure of another test.

Activity 5–11 will give you practice in analyzing causes and their effects. Read "Good Listening Is Difficult" and, on a separate sheet of paper, list seven reasons (or causes) for difficulty in listening. Conclude by explaining what the effect of poor listening skills might be on grades.

Good Listening Is Difficult

Many students would agree that listening is a difficult skill. For most, it is much harder to master new material by listening to a lecturer than by reading a textbook. Since listening, like reading, is a popular method of teaching, both in and out of school, it is important to understand why listening well is so difficult.

When listening, you have to adjust to the speed of speakers. If they speak very rapidly, you may not be able to take in all that they say. On the other hand, if they are very slow and deliberate, you may find it hard to keep your mind on what they are saying. (Your mind's pace is much more rapid than that of *any* speaker.)

You may not be mentally prepared for listening. You may not know anything about the topic and may be confused until you have heard enough to understand and focus on the subject being considered. Perhaps you don't feel well, or you are caught up in a daydream. You cannot choose the time and place for listening.

Unfortunately, there is no "replay button" to push when you are listening. If you miss what was said the first time, it is gone. You have missed it.

It is hard to be a listener and a critical thinker at the same time. When you are reading and you want to stop and consider a particular point, you can put the book aside and do so. However, when you are listening, such lengthy evaluations are not possible.

Distractions are all around you—particularly in the classroom. You may sit by a window and have a tendency to look out and watch the world. Maybe the person behind you has news about something in which you are very interested. Perhaps you would like to date the person seated across the aisle. Once your attention wanders from the speaker, it is hard to concentrate again.

Personal biases or prejudices may make it difficult for you to keep an open mind. Speaking style or physical appearance may influence the way you respond to what you hear. Listening with understanding and reserving judgment until later is difficult for most people.

The reaction of others to a topic or speaker may influence your ability to make a judgment about what the speaker is saying. Weighing the evidence and mentally keeping up with what the speaker is really saying is challenging when others have prejudged and are urging agreement.

Nevertheless, in spite of some of the roadblocks you have just read about, efficient listening in class is a skill that anyone who is committed to becoming a better listener can learn.

Active listening is a valuable study skill.

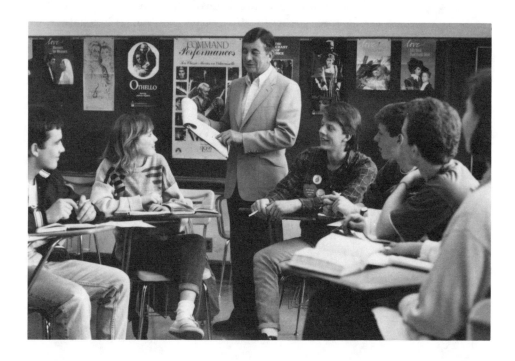

Activity 5–12
Recognizing Inferences and Drawing Conclusions

Are you a good detective? Sometimes you need to be, to understand a situation, make inferences, and draw conclusions from what you read when the results are not clearly stated.

To make inferences, you have to go beyond given words or circumstances to draw conclusions. For example, suppose you just bought a new red pen, and you are certain you left it on your desk. But the pen is missing. You find a note written in red ink by your brother. What do you infer, or what conclusions do you draw, based on your understanding of the situation?

Identifying main ideas, noting the sequence of events, visualizing the material clearly, and targeting the outcome are all skills that you have been acquiring. Now, put them to work and have some fun practicing your sleuthing as you complete the following exercises. Your goals are to understand, to make inferences, and to draw conclusions from what you read.

Begin by reading the following sentences. Then, on a separate sheet of paper, explain what conclusions you have drawn, or predict what might, will, or has happened, based on your understanding of the facts given. The first sentence has been done for you as an example.

1. Take your umbrella, as the clouds look very threatening off to the west. **Conclusion or prediction:** It might rain.

2. Yelling and booing and pointing at the referee all followed the final call.

3. It's snowing, blowing, and about two degrees above zero outside.

4. The strange creature was covered with feathers, had a long, sharp bill, and gave shrill, raucous cries when approached by the onlookers.

5. The tree was decorated, the stockings were hung, and the smell of pies baking wafted through the house.

6. The three contestants stood in a row, each nervously awaiting the spin of the wheel.

7. In spite of the deafening roar of the fans, the eleven helmeted men lined up, the referee blew the whistle, and the ball was kicked into the air.

8. The student held his breath as his paper was handed back. A quick glance at the top brought a grim expression.

9. A beaker, a few chemicals, and a loud BANG. They had done it again.

10. The hastily drawn posters were hung on the walls, the speeches were nervously given, and the votes were finally tallied. Jana smiled broadly.

Activity 5-13
Cloze

Another activity that focuses on improving your comprehension is cloze. The word *cloze* comes from the term *closure* and means to bring completion to a sentence. A cloze activity is a puzzle of sorts; you use the clues provided in the context to think of appropriate words to fill the blanks. The purpose of cloze is to teach you to use context clues to figure out the meanings of words you don't know. Cloze improves your reading comprehension, as well.

Read the following selection through first, mentally supplying the words you think belong in the spaces. Then, on a separate sheet of paper, number from one to thirty-two. Read "One Night in the Woods" again, filling in each blank with a word from the list provided. All the words in the list must be used, and some words will be used more than once. Finish by writing the word beside the appropriate number on your paper.

popped	had	trails	feet
first	the	stage	imaginary
five	imaginations	or	and
at	you	moon	enough
was	especially	tried	does
fresh	hill	a	I
prickles	crept	shadows	not

mountainside

One Night in the Woods

The fresh pine scent in the air made me glad to be out of the stuffy cabin and away from my sleeping companions. I had no flashlight, but it ___1___ just a short way up the ___2___ to the other cabin, and the ___3___ was shining. Confidently I started up ___4___ trail.

Soon I realized that it ___5___ not as bright as I had ___6___ thought. The moon slyly cast only ___7___ light to create eerie shadows. The ___8___ air rattled the aspen leaves. It ___9___ not the chilly air that caused ___10___ to crawl down my spine.

Do ___11___ know Jason? He has retired from ___12___ movie *Friday the 13th* into the ___13___ of many. Now he slithered into my thoughts. Do you know what Jason ___14___? He murders people walking up mountain ___15___ in the middle of the night, ___16___ when they are alone.

The moon ___17___ no mercy. It kept the eerie ___18___ set. "Shuuushsh," said something in the ___19___. Was it the shadow that moved ___20___ something *in* it? I shuddered and ___21___ to control my frightened thoughts.

After ___22___ more careful steps, I plainly heard ___23___ twig snap behind me. *Is* Jason ___24___? I instantly felt my heart pounding ___25___ my ribs in panic. Silent horror ___26___ to every part of my body. ___27___ could not look back. With heavy ___28___ I plodded forward.

When another twig ___29___ behind me, I froze. I was ___30___ imagining.

"BOO!" I jumped straight up ___31___ screamed. My terror resounded over the ___32___. Amy's eyes filled with tears of merriment as she exploded into giggles. After a pause I, too, began to laugh.

Activity 5–14
Unit Review

On a separate sheet of paper, answer the following questions:

I. Completion

Number from one to five. Fill in the blank with the term(s) from this unit that complete the statement.

1. The point the author is trying to get across is called the _____.

2. _____ is understanding the point the author is making.

3. Putting things in order is called _____. You must have a basic understanding in order to do this.

4. Comprehension involves understanding the relationship between _____ and effect.

5. _____ comes from the word *closure* and means to complete something. You need comprehension to bring appropriate closure to a sentence.

II. Short Essay

Read the following paragraphs. Write the number IIA and, below it, write IIB. Beside IIA write the main idea of the paragraphs. Beside IIB, list sequentially six things you can do to develop your skills as a student.

You Can Become a Better Student

There are several things you can do to become a better student. First, you can create a good study setting for yourself; where you study helps improve your concentration and comprehension.

Second, you can budget your time. Decide what subjects you need to study and in what order you should study them. Approximate how long each subject will take to study, time for breaks, and block out that amount of time in your schedule for the day.

Third, work on improving your note-taking abilities. Practice getting the main ideas down in as concise a manner as possible. Use abbreviations, personal shorthand, and a highlighter to mark the important points.

Next, develop and use good test-taking skills. Know the tricks for taking tests in general, as well as those suited to specific types of tests. Know how to handle test anxiety, how to budget your time when taking tests, and how to evaluate your test when it is returned, so that you can do better on the next test.

Fifth, understand the value of reading different material at appropriate and vastly different rates. Know when to speed up and when to slow down; know when to read at 100 words per minute and when to read at 1,000 words per minute. Then use those varying rates.

Finally, develop your listening skills. Sit away from friends, doors, windows, and other distractions. Don't prejudge speakers. Adjust to their speaking speed. And be an active listener; don't put your mind in neutral, but instead participate mentally in what the speaker is saying. Stay with that person—think about what he or she is saying.

Clearly, there are many things you can do to become a better student. Practice these techniques, and watch your grades improve.

III. Application

Choose *one* of the following (a *or* b).

a. Discuss in a brief paragraph some of the *causes* of poor grades and the *effects* poor grades may have on a student's life. Show by your discussion that you understand the cause-effect relationship.

b. Develop four inferences and demonstrate your understanding of the inferences by predicting an outcome or drawing a conclusion.

Example: Hour after hour, day after day, Luis pored over piles of notes, reviewed pages and pages in the text, and created sample test after sample test. He had to pass that final.

Prediction: Luis will pass the test because of all his preparation.

Taking notes reinforces learning.

IV. Cloze

Read the entire selection, mentally selecting the appropriate word for the blank *as* you read. Next, number from one to twenty-four. Read "Planning Your Time" again, filling in the blanks with the words from the list provided. All words in the list must be used, and some words will be used more than once. Write the appropriate word in the correct space on your answer sheet.

lower	or	project	find	should	in	of
pays	your	the	last	for	are	
time	employer	search	sight	take	as	

Planning Your Time

Even if you are under no economic pressure to find a job quickly, starting your search promptly is a wise policy. Delays may hurt your chances of finding the job you want. If you have just finished school, for example, you __1__ competing for similar positions with other new graduates in __2__ field. Moreover, a long delay between school or your __3__ job and your application for work may give an __4__ the impression that his or her office is one __5__ your last stops in a long and fruitless job __6__.

Once you start your search, you should treat it __7__ a full-time job. Set realistic goals and keep __8__ of them. It is important to remember that looking __9__ work can be discouraging. Do not let employer rejections __10__ your self-esteem or serve as an excuse to "__11__ a vacation" from job seeking. Sustained effort usually __12__ off.

The following suggestions may help you plan your __13__ for an efficient job search:

1. Plan and start your __14__ as soon as you know you will need to __15__ a new job.

2. Make your job hunting a full-time __16__. You work a 40-hour week for your employer; you __17__ work no less for yourself.

3. Once you start your __18__, do not allow yourself little vacations.

4. Apply early enough __19__ the day to allow time for multiple interviews, tests, __20__ other hiring procedures that may be required.

5. Be on __21__ for appointments.

6. Before approaching a firm, try to learn __22__ best time and day of the week to apply __23__ a job.

7. Follow up leads immediately. If you learn __24__ a job opening late in the day, call the firm to arrange an appointment for the next day. The employer may postpone a hiring decision until then.

Increasing Speed

INCREASE (ĭn-krēs'), v. to make or become greater or larger

SPEED (spēd), n. a rate of performance; swiftness of action

Are you reading as well or as fast as you might? If not, don't despair—you are not alone! Most students receive no formal training in the "how to's" of reading after late grade school. It is not surprising, then, that you may feel your skills don't meet the demands now being made on them.

Some students read everything at the same slow rate in order to have maximum understanding of what they have read. But problems come when their reading speed is slow enough to allow daydreaming.

Whatever your reading rates, remember that speed and comprehension go hand in hand. Read too slowly, and daydreaming sets in; read too fast, and little or nothing stays in your memory.

With practice and determination, you can improve your reading speed and comprehension.

The information and exercises in Unit 6 will help you improve your reading speed—an area many students find to be a problem, no matter what the subject matter. If you are determined, and if you can exercise self-discipline, you can eliminate some inefficient reading habits that serve as barriers to your success.

Reading rates are very personal. It is not important to compare your speed with that of another. What *is* important is that *you* are reading faster, comprehending more, and remembering longer. The final payoff will be in better understanding of the material and improved grades.

Activities 6–1 Through 6–10
Rapid Discrimination Drills

Reading at a speed that is too slow leads to boredom and daydreaming because your brain is not challenged. If you find yourself daydreaming as you read, perhaps you need to try reading faster. Use the rapid discrimination drills in Activities 6–1 through 6–10 to push yourself to read more quickly.

The drills will help you increase your reading speed because they force you to look at words and pick out, at very rapid rates, those that are alike or different. The drills will train you to recognize word meanings quickly. In addition, they will challenge you to take in longer and longer words at the same rapid rate in which you recognize the shorter words. To use the drills, follow this procedure:

1. Label the upper righthand corner of a separate sheet of paper as shown:

	Min.	Sec.
Time stopped	_____	_____
Time began	_____	_____
Total time read	_____	_____

2. Number your paper from one to twenty.

If your instructor is timing the drill:

3. Listen carefully to instructions and do not begin working until your instructor gives you the signal.

4. Look up when you finish and record the total time you read based on the time card being held by your instructor.

5. Correct your paper as your instructor gives the answers, and record the total time you read and your score on the chart you construct. (See the model chart at the end of this introduction.)

If your instructor is not timing the drill, use the following procedure:

3. Using a watch or clock with a second hand, note the time you begin on your sheet of paper.

4. Turn to the proper page, read the instructions at the top of that page, and complete the drill as quickly as possible.

5. Note the time you finish. Subtract the time you began from the time you finished to determine the total time you read. Grade your paper using the answer key in the appendix at the end of this unit. Then, compute your score by giving yourself five points for each correct answer; record your score on a chart like the one shown below.

Remember: Your goal is to improve or maintain your reading time and score while increasing the length of the words you are reading. To benefit most from these drills, practice them on four consecutive days, using three sequential exercises each day.

RAPID DISCRIMINATION DRILLS

		1	2	3	4	5	6	7	8	9	10
Different Word	Time										
	Score										
Same Word	Time										
	Score										
Meaning	Time										
	Score										

Activity 6-1
Rapid Discrimination Drill #1
Write the number of the word that is different.

	1	2	3	4	5
1.	site	site	site	side	site
2.	cord	cord	cord	cord	card
3.	nail	mail	nail	nail	nail
4.	maps	maps	naps	maps	maps
5.	pore	pore	pore	pore	bore
6.	raid	paid	paid	paid	paid
7.	look	look	book	look	look
8.	cake	rake	rake	rake	rake
9.	pear	tear	pear	pear	pear
10.	cook	cook	cook	took	cook
11.	felt	felt	felt	felt	melt

12. cape	cape	tape	cape	cape
13. jack	rack	rack	rack	rack
14. veil	veil	veil	veal	veil
15. hats	rats	hats	hats	hats
16. jump	jump	jump	jump	pump
17. pale	pale	dale	pale	pale
18. pool	pool	pool	poor	pool
19. tool	took	took	took	took
20. cart	part	cart	cart	cart

Activity 6–2
Rapid Discrimination Drill #2

A **key word** is given. Write the number of the space in which it is repeated.

Key Word	1	2	3	4	5
1. dull	mull	pull	full	dull	cull
2. desk	mask	deck	pest	desk	risk
3. last	mast	last	past	task	fast
4. mask	mope	task	mask	make	made
5. made	raid	fade	paid	jade	made
6. rail	mail	tail	sail	rail	pail
7. hook	hook	took	book	look	cook
8. rule	mule	rule	tool	fool	cool
9. hope	rope	Pope	lope	nope	hope
10. took	took	cook	look	rook	book
11. bone	tone	moan	hone	bone	loan
12. clad	paid	made	fade	glad	clad
13. dirt	curt	tart	dirt	mart	bard
14. feel	meal	zeal	real	feel	peal
15. boat	moat	boat	coat	tote	goat
16. jeer	mere	fear	jeer	tear	leer
17. pony	pony	home	bone	tone	zone
18. real	peal	meal	teal	real	seal
19. pare	bare	mare	tare	fare	pare
20. belt	belt	felt	melt	pelt	welt

Activity 6–3
Rapid Discrimination Drill #3
List the number of the word(s) that mean(s) the same as the **key word**.

Key Word	1	2	3	4
1. site	hill	scene	place	land
2. spry	old	smart	active	thin
3. rely	ask	depend	expect	balk
4. balk	trip	fall	stop short	frighten
5. bask	play	sun	warm oneself	fry
6. vows	wish	promises	order	command
7. clue	hint	reminder	thought	answer
8. ajar	wide open	unlocked	closed	partly open
9. burr	rough edge	haircut	dig deep	sandy shore
10. hint	answer	slight sign	explanation	essay
11. vary	shrink	increase	grow	change
12. feat	foolish	skillful act	trip	flight
13. chat	speech	easy talk	explanation	lecture
14. chef	cook	dean	president	policeman
15. clad	completely	appearing	dressed	working
16. poll	campaign	question	debate	vote
17. pant	behave	slight	short breath	enough
18. odor	neither	smell	danger	taste
19. rein	rain	reign	bridle strap	razor
20. heir	session	who inherits	hair	ancestor

Activity 6–4
Rapid Discrimination Drill #4
Write the number of the word that is different.

	1	2	3	4	5
1.	blurt	flirt	flirt	flirt	flirt
2.	power	power	flour	power	power
3.	medal	metal	medal	medal	medal
4.	align	align	align	alien	align
5.	check	check	check	check	cheek
6.	burly	curly	burly	burly	burly
7.	abide	chide	chide	chide	chide
8.	flood	flood	flood	flood	blood
9.	trunk	trunk	trunk	chunk	trunk
10.	plush	plush	blush	plush	plush
11.	glaze	craze	craze	craze	craze
12.	twist	twist	twist	twist	wrist
13.	float	float	floor	float	float
14.	shade	shade	shade	shape	shade
15.	widow	width	widow	widow	widow
16.	hazy	hazy	crazy	hazy	hazy
17.	blush	plush	plush	plush	plush
18.	pedal	pedal	pedal	medal	pedal
19.	chase	chute	chase	chase	chase
20.	shame	shame	shame	shame	share

Activity 6–5
Rapid Discrimination Drill #5

A **key word** is given. Write the number of the space in which it is repeated.

Key Word	1	2	3	4	5
1. bonus	tones	bonus	cones	hones	phone
2. shame	share	shout	shoot	shore	shame
3. write	trite	sight	write	fight	white
4. weigh	weigh	worry	neigh	wrist	wring
5. glass	glare	globe	glaze	glass	gland
6. blunt	blunt	bloom	bloat	blown	black
7. dingy	diner	dingy	dings	dinky	dingo
8. wield	yield	field	wield	wierd	waist
9. gland	gloom	glove	glory	glass	gland
10. wrist	twist	crust	wisps	wrist	grist
11. block	blare	block	blast	blank	blame
12. false	fable	faint	famed	false	fancy
13. boils	boils	toils	foils	coils	bowls
14. aides	maids	raids	aides	paids	fades
15. chase	chaff	chair	chain	chalk	chase
16. legal	legal	leach	leafy	leaky	learn
17. rebel	ready	rebel	realm	recur	reign
18. champ	chalk	chair	champ	chain	chaff
19. agent	again	agaze	agent	agile	aging
20. brief	brick	bribe	bride	brief	briar

Activity 6–6
Rapid Discrimination Drill #6

List the number of the word(s) that mean(s) the same as the **key word**.

Key Word	1	2	3	4
1. vocal	of voice	simple	harmonizing	loud
2. drawl	slow talk	fast talk	quiet talk	loud talk
3. elude	hide from	void	evade	discover
4. array	table	menu	amount	display
5. scent	choke	odor	sent	mail
6. sheer	very thin	shore	clean	cut
7. adapt	to learn	to modify	to probe	to notify
8. tempt	tame	test	threaten	trust
9. realm	flavor	kingdom	pilot	reality
10. agony	uncertain	pain	acute	scholar
11. amuse	entertain	harp	ignorance	abuse
12. alter	additional	graduate	altar	change
13. prong	sharp edge	blade	pointed end	pin
14. valet	housekeeper	cook	gardener	servant
15. abode	dwelling	atmosphere	situation	surrounding
16. foyer	basement	office	porch	entry hall
17. horde	swarm	trace	rodent	family
18. solar	of planets	of stars	of sun	of universe
19. wield	lift up	accomplish	obtain	hold and use
20. vivid	empty	cold	alive	dull blue

Activity 6–7
Rapid Discrimination Drill #7
Write the number of the word that is different.

	1	2	3	4	5
1.	belong	belief	belong	belong	belong
2.	census	census	census	censor	census
3.	facing	facing	facial	facing	facing
4.	agency	agenda	agenda	agenda	agenda
5.	device	device	device	device	devise
6.	tender	hinder	tender	tender	tender
7.	liking	liking	liking	likely	liking
8.	pardon	parent	parent	parent	parent
9.	jacket	jacket	racket	jacket	jacket
10.	triple	triple	triple	triple	ripple
11.	shrewd	shreds	shreds	shreds	shreds
12.	thresh	thresh	thrash	thresh	thresh
13.	reboil	recoil	reboil	reboil	reboil
14.	series	series	serial	series	series
15.	reform	reform	reform	reflex	reform
16.	snatch	snitch	snitch	snitch	snitch
17.	status	status	status	status	static
18.	gratis	gravel	gratis	gratis	gratis
19.	hooded	hooded	hooves	hooded	hooded
20.	tingle	tingle	tingle	mingle	tingle

Activity 6–8
Rapid Discrimination Drill #8
A **key word** is given. Write the number of the space in which it is repeated.

Key Word	1	2	3	4	5
1. modify	module	modest	modify	modern	models
2. nibble	pebble	treble	nimble	normal	nibble
3. pellet	pellet	mallet	ballet	market	target
4. rescue	resale	resume	resort	rescue	resist
5. sadden	saddle	sadden	sadder	sadism	sacred
6. spider	spinet	spinal	spiral	spider	spirit
7. broken	broken	broach	broker	bronze	brooms
8. change	chance	cancel	change	chapel	charge
9. commit	combat	comely	comets	common	commit
10. damper	damsel	damper	dampen	damask	damage
11. gamble	gander	gamble	gargle	garlic	garret
12. indent	indeed	indebt	indict	indent	indoor
13. jangle	jangle	jingle	jargon	jaunty	jersey
14. misuse	miscue	misery	misuse	misfit	mishap
15. oppose	option	oracle	orbits	orphan	oppose
16. radial	radios	radial	radium	radius	random
17. seaman	season	seater	secede	seaman	second
18. hubbub	hubbub	hugged	humble	humans	hunger
19. limber	linger	lining	limber	liquid	listen
20. memory	method	mental	midget	member	memory

Activity 6–9
Rapid Discrimination Drill #9
List the number of the word (s) that mean(s) the same as the **key word.**

Key Word	1	2	3	4
1. rustic	rural	rusty	normal	simple
2. hectic	dramatic	dull	very busy	angry
3. deluge	sprinkle	shower	heavy rain	fog
4. relish	care	speed	amusement	enjoy
5. defect	stowaway	noise	fault	repair
6. sultry	hot and humid	sunny	overcast	smelly
7. relent	soften	lend	surrender	hold firm
8. smudge	would	expression	dirt	smear
9. caress	lick	stroke	protect	warm
10. heroic	strong	loyal	friendly	brave
11. tremor	loud noise	shaking	shock	frighten
12. stench	stretch	dirty	stingy	bad smell
13. differ	be like	be unlike	be kind	be common
14. decree	infant	circular	rejoice	royal law
15. hatred	flush	great dislike	hurt	sacred
16. bestow	best one	give	take	put away
17. offend	kettle	ladder	often	make angry
18. define	settler	legal	state meaning	defend
19. emerge	lead on	come out	dispute	image
20. induce	bring about	enclose	sight	intrude

Activity 6–10
Rapid Discrimination Drill #10
Write the number of the word that is different.

	1	2	3	4	5
1.	baggage	bagpipe	bagpipe	bagpipe	bagpipe
2.	calcify	calcify	calcium	calcify	calcify
3.	dogwood	dolphin	dogwood	dogwood	dogwood
4.	flatcar	flatcar	flatcar	flatcar	flatten
5.	grating	grating	grating	gratify	grating
6.	hemline	hemlock	hemline	hemline	hemline
7.	illegal	illicit	illicit	illicit	illicit
8.	inverse	inverse	invalid	inverse	inverse
9.	justify	justify	justify	justify	justice
10.	kinetic	kinetic	kinetic	kindred	kinetic
11.	lapsing	larceny	lapsing	lapsing	lapsing
12.	martial	marshal	marshal	marshal	marshal
13.	nitrite	nitrite	nitrate	nitrite	nitrite
14.	offices	offices	offices	offices	officer
15.	plastic	plastic	plastic	plaster	plastic
16.	rampage	rampage	rampage	rampant	rampage
17.	recruit	rectify	recruit	recruit	recruit
18.	secular	section	section	section	section
19.	spastic	spastic	sparkle	spastic	spastic
20.	tipster	tipster	tipster	tipster	timeout

Activity 6–11
Timed Readings

Being creatures of habit, it is easy to fall into the pattern of reading everything at the most comfortable rate. But that isn't an efficient way to read. Instead, you should vary your rate to suit your purpose, the difficulty of the material, and your background. Sometimes this means reading, without sacrificing comprehension, as quickly as you can. Of course, learning to read more rapidly takes practice, just like anything else at which you want to improve.

One easy way to increase reading speed is to read a lot. Choose the type of material that interests you. In order to focus your attention on improving your reading speed, try this method of timed readings two or three times per week over a period of weeks.

1. Write the following on a separate sheet of paper.

number of lines read	____(1)____
× number of words per line	(2)
total number of words read	____(3)____
total number of words read	____(4)____
÷ number of minutes read	(5)
rate in words per minute	____(6)____

2. Select an article or chapter that interests you.

3. Before starting to read, determine the average number of words per line in the selection you have chosen. To do this, count all the words in 10 lines and divide by 10 for the average number of words per line. Write this number on your sheet of paper in Space 2.
Number of words in 10 lines ÷ by 10 = average number of words per line

If your instructor is timing, you will be told when to begin reading, and when to stop.
If your instructor is not timing, you will need a watch with a second hand, or a timer.

4. Do two timed readings whenever you practice. Read each time for the same number of minutes. (We suggest three to six minutes per reading.)

5. Set a timer and begin reading at a comfortable rate. When the timer signals that your reading time is finished, note on your paper in Space 5 the number of minutes you read. Then mark your place in the material you read.

6. Count the number of lines you read and write this down in Space 1.

7. Figure the number of words per minute you read by multiplying the total number of lines (Space 1) by the average number of words per line (Space 2).

8. Column Two: Divide the total number of words you read (Space 3 or 4) by the number of minutes you read (Space 5). This figure will be the number of words per minute (wpm) that you read (Space 6).

Example:

1.	number of lines read	100
2.	number of words per line	$\times$ 6
3.	total number of words read	600
4.	total number of words read	600
5.	number of minutes read	$\div$ 3
6.	rate in words per minute	200

For your second timed reading, continue from where you finished before, pushing yourself to read as quickly as you can without losing comprehension. (This may seem awkward at first.) When your time is up, again compute your words read per minute using the same formula as before.

Record both your comfortable rate and your "push" rate on a chart you make on a separate sheet of paper. Use the following chart as an example.

Speed-reading Chart

Date	Number of words/line	Number of lines	Number of minutes	Rate in words per minute
9/21	6	100	3	200

As you continue with your timed reading practices during class, you will see progress if you are serious about wanting to read faster. Be sure to compare the differences between your comfortable rates and your push rates, as well as noting your increases in reading speed.

Additional Activities to Increase Reading Speed[1]

There are several other activities you can do to improve your reading speed. You will need light, easy, and enjoyable reading material; choose something you look forward to reading. Make up your mind that you will push yourself beyond your normal reading rate; you will be surprised at how soon the new reading speed becomes comfortable for you.

Decide how much time you can spend on an activity and then select a drill from the suggestions that follow.

One-Minute Speed Drills

This drill resembles the timed readings discussed previously. Read for one minute, determine your rate in words per minute, and record it on your Speed-reading Chart. Then read for another minute, trying to beat your previous score. Do this for ten minutes several times a week.

One-Page Speed Drills

In this drill you read one page at a time and work for improvement. Note the time before you begin reading, read the page, and note the time upon ending reading. Try another one-page reading in an attempt to improve your previous time. Repeat this process two or three times a week.

Ten-Page Speed Drills

Count out ten pages and mark the tenth page with a paper clip. Note the time and begin reading. Push yourself. At the end of the tenth page, note the time again and determine how many minutes you spent reading. Record this time; it is this time you want to improve when you repeat the exercise with ten other pages. Try to practice.

One-Hour Speed Drills

Note the time and read for one hour. Count the number of pages you read. Your goal is to read more pages the next time you read for an hour using similar material.

One-Book Speed Drills

This drill is for avid readers. Determine the number of hours it takes you to read a book (approximately). Then divide the number of pages in a book you wish to read by the number of hours it usually takes you to finish reading.

Example: 200 pages in 4 hours = 50 pages per hour

Put a paper clip on the page you should reach after one hour of reading. Set the timer for one hour. Then, at the end of that hour, count how many pages you read and record the results. Repeat the process using the hourly page rate you accomplished in your most recent drill as the rate you want to improve on.

[1] The activities offered to increase reading speed are from *Improving Reading in Every Class* by Ellen Lamar Thomas and H. Alan Robinson, and *Reading Aids for Every Class* by Ellen Lamar Thomas. Both books were published by Allyn & Bacon, Inc., Boston.

Activities 6–12 Through 6–15
Speed and Comprehension Drills

Improving your reading speed is of no value if your comprehension doesn't keep up. Comprehension—how well you understand and recognize important points in what you read—is essential to your success as a student.

In Activities 6–12 through 6–15, you will be asked to read several articles at a speed that will ensure 70 percent comprehension, or better. As you read, you will learn about reading rates, the process of reading, poor reading habits, and developing a good vocabulary. Ten questions follow each article, to help you evaluate your comprehension skills.

If your instructor is not timing these exercises, you will need a watch, clock, or timer. Time yourself, and record your time. Your goal is to improve your time—even as the activities get longer. After you read, answer the questions, and check your paper for comprehension errors using the answer key in the Appendix at the end of this unit. Score your work by adding a zero to the number correct. Then, on a separate sheet of paper, make a chart entitled "Comprehension Activities" like the one that follows, and record your time and score.

Comprehension Activities

	1	2	3	4	5	6	7	8	9	10
Time										
Score										

Activity 6–12
Speed and Comprehension Drill #1

Read "What Is Your Reading Rate?" and answer the questions that follow the article. Time yourself, or ask your instructor to time you. Record your time on your Comprehension Activities chart.

What Is Your Reading Rate?

If someone asks you "What is your reading rate?" you can be sure that person knows very little about reading. It is incorrect to assume a person has just *one* reading rate. Although research shows the average high school student reads at an average of 250 words per minute, the really good reader knows reading rates need to be *flexible*.

Some students think that, if they read everything slowly, they will achieve maximum comprehension. However, they are wrong. In fact, sometimes reading so slowly has the opposite effect because it lulls those people into daydreaming and boredom. Their brains are not being challenged. Successful readers learn to read quickly when it is warranted and slowly when it is necessary.

So, what determines the correct reading speed? Three factors determine it. The first is the difficulty of the material. If the material you are reading is complex, you must slow your reading speed. If the material is easy and entertaining, you can speed up your reading. The second factor is purpose. *Why* are you reading the material? If you are reading it to prepare for a quiz the next day, you'd better slow your pace. If you are reading it for pleasure, then you can speed up. Finally, the third factor that determines reading speed is familiarity with the subject matter. If the material and the concepts are new to you, then slow down your reading to take them in. If you are already familiar with the concepts in the material, then speed up. Good readers learn to vary their speed from 150 to 800 words per minute, choosing their appropriate speed after considering all three factors: difficulty, purpose, and familiarity.

Number from one to ten on a separate sheet of paper. Beside each number write *true* if the statement is true and *false* if the statement is false.

1. Everyone has *one* personal reading rate.

2. High-school students read an average of 250 words per minute.

3. Reading slowly assures a student of maximum comprehension.

4. The difficulty of the material is a consideration when choosing a reading rate.

5. A very difficult selection should be read at 250 words per minute.

6. A light, entertaining selection should be read at 250 words per minute.

7. Almost everyone reads material for a quiz at a slower speed than material for relaxation.

8. An astronomy expert can probably read an article on astronomy at a faster rate than someone who knows nothing about the subject.

9. Before selecting your own reading rate, you should consider the average reading rate of others in your class.

10. One of the major points made in this unit is that reading rates must be constantly changing.

Activity 6–13

Speed and Comprehension Drill #2

Read the article entitled "How Do You Read?" and answer the questions that follow it. Time yourself, or ask your instructor to time you. Then record your time.

How Do You Read?

Most students probably assume that when they read, their eyes follow in a straight motion across the lines of print, like this:

Eyes follow the print in a straight line.

That is not so. You need only to sit across from someone and carefully observe his or her reading process to discover:

The eyes move in an arc across the lines of print.

Each time the eyes reach the bottom of the arc, they pause, or stop to take in words. These pauses are called *fixations*. It is only at the fixation point that your eyes see words. When the eye is making the arc, the motion is rapid; in fact, it is so rapid, the reader is unaware of it. Only your brain "sees" the rapid blur of the arc. It's fortunate that as you read you do not see the arc—it would cause a terrible headache! As your eyes go through the motions of reading, they are in the arc 6 percent of the time; 94 percent is spent at the points of fixation.

Slow readers move their eyes in the word-by-word arc illustrated above. It is easy to see why slow readers tire easily and become discouraged. Reading is a difficult process for them.

Fast readers, on the other hand, read more fluently.

Fast readers take in 2.5 to 3 words per fixation, making the task of reading a much simpler one. Our goal in this unit is to use the rapid discrimination exercises as beginning drills to expand the amount of letters, and then words, you can take in per fixation. You begin with as few as four *letters* per fixation. With practice, you can work up to 2.5 to 3 *words* per fixation. This skill will help you be a better reader, and will save you time, as well.

Number from one to ten on a separate sheet of paper. Beside each number write *true* if the statement is true and *false* if the statement is false.

1. A fixation is a pause or stop of the eyes to take in words.

2. A reader's eyes do not move in a straight line when reading.

3. Fifty percent of a reader's time is spent in motion between words, and 50 percent is spent fixating.

4. An inefficient or slow reader takes in one word per fixation.

5. An efficient reader takes in four to five words per fixation.

6. The eyes of a slow reader make an arc every 2.5 to 3 words.

7. The eyes of an efficient reader make an arc covering one word at a time.

8. Readers are aware of the blur made when their eyes make the arc motion from one fixation to the next.

9. The blur made by the arc motion causes some people to get frequent headaches when reading.

10. There is no difference between the amount of effort a slow reader puts forth while reading and the amount of effort a fast reader puts forth.

Activity 6–14
Speed and Comprehension Drill #3

Read the following article and answer the questions. Time yourself, or ask your instructor to time you. Then record your time; are you improving?

Reading Habits That Slow You Down

As you work to build your reading speed, you must consider four common reading habits.

The first, *vocalizing*, is mouthing or saying the words aloud as you read them. It is easy to spot someone who has this problem. And vocalizing *is* a problem, because the act of mouthing or speaking slows you down; it takes too much time to say the words with your lips. There are several ways to help yourself stop vocalizing. Try chewing gum or holding a pencil clenched between your teeth as you read. Or, put your hand over your mouth or keep it at your throat to feel for vibrations of vocalizing.

Unfortunately, the second problem reading habit is much harder to detect. It is called *subvocalizing*, and it is characterized by a reader's forming the words in his or her larynx. In order to avoid pronouncing internally the words you read, practice reading rapidly under timed conditions, or talk about the material to yourself.

The third problem reading habit is *pointing*. When you point with your finger or a pencil or a ruler, you add another mechanical step to the reading process. This can only slow you down. The solution is to make pointing impossible by folding your hands in your lap.

The last problem reading habit is *head movement*. Following the lines of print with your head does not increase reading speed. Like pointing, it adds another mechanical step to the reading process. To avoid it, hold your chin in your hand, or place your hand against the side of your head.

Of course, there are other reading problems that affect reading speed, but these four are common. Each can be diagnosed fairly easily, though, and corrected with practice over time.

Point only when you *need* to slow down your reading rate, such as when you are checking lists or answers.

Number from one to ten on a separate sheet of paper. Beside each number write *true* if the statement is true and *false* if the statement is false.

1. *Vocalizing* is mouthing the words when reading.

2. Vocalizing does not slow down a reader's speed; it just distracts others.

3. Chewing gum while reading is a cure for vocalizing.

4. Subvocalizing is like vocalizing; the words are said aloud for everyone to hear.

5. Reading rapidly under timed conditions is a cure for subvocalizing.

6. Pointing with your finger helps you keep your place and improves your reading speed.

7. Pointing with a pencil or ruler is preferred to pointing with a finger.

8. Moving your head to follow the lines of print slows your reading speed.

9. A cure for head movement is to hold your hand against the side of your head as you read, so that you can feel any head movement.

10. There are only four reading problems people need to consider.

Activity 6–15
Speed and Comprehension Drill #4

Read the article entitled "Vocabulary Affects Speed and Comprehension" and answer the questions that follow. Time yourself, or ask your instructor to time you. Record your time, then compare it to your time on the first drill.

Vocabulary Affects Speed and Comprehension

The previous comprehension activity focused on four common reading problems that affect reading speed. A fifth problem is a poor vocabulary. If you stumble over words, or you have to stop and think about them, your reading speed is slowed. Developing a good vocabulary will help you to improve both your reading speed and your comprehension.

One way to improve your vocabulary is to read a lot. The more you read, the more words you'll encounter, and the more your vocabulary will grow.

You can also improve your vocabulary by paying attention to new words. Instead of skipping over it, stop and figure out what a new word means. Use context clues from the sentence, if possible.

If context clues don't help, look up the meaning of the word in your dictionary. Then make a special effort to learn it. Using the new word in your writing or conversations will help you remember it.

Keeping a vocabulary notebook will also help. Although writing down the new words and their meanings takes more time, the benefits to you will make your extra efforts well worthwhile.

If possible, get involved in an organized vocabulary program in class. Use a vocabulary workbook and complete at least one lesson per week. Your vocabulary will grow if you make a genuine effort to learn and use the words in each lesson.

Finally, become aware of root words, prefixes, and suffixes. In *Speed-reading for Better Grades*, Ward Cramer states it is possible to double your vocabulary by learning no more than a couple dozen prefixes.

Of course, the key to developing your vocabulary is by *being aware* of new words, by *discovering* their meanings, by *committing* them to memory, and by *using* them in your conversations.

Number from one to ten on a separate sheet of paper. Beside each number write *true* if the statement is true and *false* if the statement is false.

1. Developing a good vocabulary will help your reading speed, but not your comprehension.

2. The more you read, the more your vocabulary will grow.

3. Using clues within a sentence to determine the meaning of a word will help increase your vocabulary.

4. Context clues are the clues to a word's meaning given by the sentence or paragraph in which the word appears.

5. The process of looking up a word's definition in the dictionary is sufficient for learning that word.

6. Using a new word in your conversation with others does not help you learn the word.

7. Keeping a vocabulary notebook takes too much time, and the payoffs aren't worth it.

8. Completing lessons in a vocabulary workbook pays off in an increased vocabulary.

9. Learning a couple dozen prefixes will double your vocabulary.

10. Learning root words is a waste of time for vocabulary building.

Activity 6–16
Unit Review

Answer the following on a separate sheet of paper.
I. True–False
    Number your paper from one to ten. Read the following statements.
    Write *true* if the statement is true or *false* if the statement is false.

1. A knowledgeable and efficient reader reads all materials at the same rate.

2. Reading rate is not affected by having a good vocabulary or a poor one.

3. One way to build a good vocabulary is to read a lot.

4. You can build a good vocabulary by using the dictionary to look up meanings of words you don't know.

5. One way to build a good vocabulary is to use new words frequently in writing and conversations.

6. To build a good vocabulary, you should skip over a word you don't know, unless it appears more than once in your reading.

7. To build a good vocabulary, keep a vocabulary notebook.

8. Learning common prefixes, suffixes, and roots of words can help you build your vocabulary.

9. Your eyes move in a straight line across the lines of print as you read.

10. Reading rates are much the same from one person to the next.

II. Multiple-Choice
    Number your paper from eleven to fourteen. Place the letter of the correct answer beside the corresponding number on your paper.

11. Reading speed is determined by which of the following:

A. your purpose.
B. your background.
C. the level of difficulty.
D. A, B, and C

12. A *fixation* is a pause or stop of the eyes to take in words as you read. How many words does a slow reader take in at one fixation?
A. one
B. two
C. three
D. none of these

13. How many words does a fast reader take in at one fixation?
A. one
B. one to two
C. two or more
D. none of these

14. How many words does an efficient reader take in at one fixation?
A. 1.0 to 1.5
B. 2.0 to 2.5
C. 2.5 to 3.0
D. none of these

III. Matching

Four common reading faults are listed in the left-hand column, and cures for each are listed in the right column below. Number your paper from fifteen to twenty-one. Choose the cure(s) for each fault and write the answer(s) beside the correct number on your paper.

15 to 16. Vocalization (pronouncing each word)—Two cures

17 to 18. Subvocalization (nothing visible; words are formed in the larynx)—Two cures

19 to 20. Head movement—Two cures

21. Pointing with finger, pencil, or pen—One cure

A. Fold your hands and let your eyes do the work.

B. Place your hand against the side of your head.

C. Chew gum as you read.

D. Talk about the problem to yourself.

E. Hold a pencil clenched between your teeth.

F. Read rapidly under timed conditions.

G. Hold your chin firmly in your hand.

H. None of the above.

IV. Short Essay

22. Discuss the value of the rapid discrimination drills and whether they have helped you. If they have helped, explain how; if they haven't, explain why not.

23. Discuss what you learned in Unit 6 about reading speed (and comprehension). How can you apply this knowledge to your own reading skills?

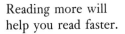

Reading more will help you read faster.

Appendix
Answers to Rapid Discrimination Drills 1 to 10

Activity #:	1	2	3	4	5	6	7	8	9	10
Question #: 1	4	4	2	1	2	1	2	3	4	1
2	5	4	3	3	5	1	4	5	3	3
3	2	2	2	2	3	3	3	1	3	2
4	3	3	3	4	1	4	1	4	4	5
5	5	5	3	5	4	2	5	2	3	4
6	1	4	2	2	1	1	2	4	1	2
7	3	1	1	1	2	2	4	1	1	1
8	1	2	4	5	3	2	1	3	4	3
9	2	5	1	4	5	2	3	5	2	5
10	4	1	2	3	4	2	5	2	4	4
11	5	4	4	1	2	1	1	2	2	2
12	3	5	2	5	4	4	3	4	4	1
13	1	3	2	3	1	3	2	1	2	3
14	4	4	1	4	3	4	3	3	4	5
15	2	2	3	2	5	1	4	5	2	4
16	5	3	2	3	1	4	1	2	2	4
17	3	1	3	1	2	1	5	4	4	2
18	4	4	2	4	3	3	2	1	3	1
19	1	5	3	2	3	4	3	3	2	3
20	2	1	2	5	4	3	4	5	1	5

Activities 6–12 to 6–15
Answers to Comprehension Questions 1 to 4

Activity #:		6–12	6–13	6–14	6–15
Question #:	1	false	true	true	false
	2	true	true	false	true
	3	false	false	true	true
	4	true	true	false	true
	5	false	false	true	false
	6	false	false	false	false
	7	true	false	false	false
	8	true	false	true	true
	9	false	false	true	true
	10	true	false	false	false

UNIT SEVEN

Skimming and Scanning

SKIM (skĭm) v. to read or glance through quickly or superficially

SCAN (skăn) v. to check carefully for a specific piece of information

ou already have been introduced to the idea that you read different materials at different rates of speed. For example, you would not read *Mad* Magazine at the same speed that you would read a letter from a lawyer about an inheritance from a distant aunt. Different speeds should be used for different purposes when reading. If you are reading everything at the same rate, you are wasting your time!

Unit 7 focuses on the range of your reading rates. Do you read at speeds of 100 to 200 words per minute (wpm)? Do you think you can read at speeds of close to 1,000 wpm? You are about to discover the answers to these questions.

You will begin with a slow and careful rate and advance through the rapid and very rapid rates achieved in skimming and scanning. The range of your reading rates may surprise you.

Activity 7–1
Flexible Reading Rates

First, you need to be aware that there *are* different reading rates. You may be surprised at just how flexible your own reading rates are presently. For instance, without realizing it, you probably use different rates to skim the newspaper and scan the phone book than you use to read this textbook.

On a separate sheet of paper, begin a section of notes entitled "Skimming and Scanning." Read the selection "Reading Rates Should Be Flexible," and answer these questions. *Remember*: For better memory retention and recall, be sure to write *both* the questions and the answers.

Skimming and Scanning

1. What three things determine your reading rate?

2. What is *scanning*? When should you use it?

3. What is *skimming*? When should you use it?

4. When should you use a rate that is rapid? very rapid? average? slow and careful?

5. What two factors influence reading rates?

Reading Rates Should Be Flexible

If someone asks you "What is your reading speed?" you can assume that he or she doesn't know much about reading. Reading everything fast or slow is the sign of a poor reader. If you are a good reader, you have several different reading rates.

A good reader shifts from one rate to another according to the following considerations:

1. What is the *purpose* of your reading? Are you studying or reading for pleasure? Are you getting a general overview, or are you looking for specific facts?

2. How *difficult* is the material to comprehend? Is it hard or easy for you to read the selection?

3. How *familiar* is the subject matter to you? Is this all new material or do you have some background in the subject?

Good readers use many different rates. If you have never thought about this, you will be surprised to learn that good readers switch from one rate to another as they need to. No conscious thought process is used; they just switch automatically.

Let's consider the rates involved in skimming and scanning. In *skimming*, you get an overview or hit only the major points of the material. You read the first few paragraphs, then glance over the remaining material, noting the chapter headings and words in bold type. Skimming is useful for getting acquainted with a new text, for choosing suitable reference material for a report, or for selecting a book from the library. Your skimming rates might range from 800 to 1,000 words per minute (wpm).

In *scanning*, you glance at material until you find a particular piece of information. When you look for a telephone number, or you find a

particular date in a history book chapter full of dates, you scan. Your scanning rate might be 1,000 to 1,500 wpm or more.

Clearly, skimming and scanning are valuable skills for you to acquire. They have many practical uses.

Your range of reading rates will include the following:

1. Very rapid—perhaps 400 wpm. Used for light, entertaining reading, such as fast-moving fiction.

2. Rapid—perhaps 350 wpm. Used for fairly easy material from which you need only the more important facts.

3. Average—perhaps 250 wpm. Used for most of the material read in daily life and for some school work.

4. Slow and careful—perhaps 200 down to 50 wpm. Used for thorough reading, to remember details, difficult concepts, and vocabulary.

You may need to shift from one reading rate to another within the same article or chapter. Good readers can do it without even thinking about it. For example, you might read the beginning of an article at an average rate, as you are being introduced to its contents. But as you proceed, a step-by-step technique is outlined, and you would switch to a slow and careful rate to increase your memory retention. At the end of the article, the author might restate the major points covered. Again you would shift gears, returning to an average or fairly rapid reading rate, depending on your familiarity with the material.

Remember that your reading rates are extremely personal. Although you may have a variety of rates that you have learned to use easily, the speeds you can attain are not the same as those of another person. Temperament and intelligence also influence reading rates.

Activity 7–2
Skimming and Scanning

In Activity 7–1 you were introduced to the concepts of skimming and scanning. You may have been surprised to find that you already use these techniques in your everyday life, without even thinking about it. But do you use these same tools in your academic pursuits? If you do not, you are wasting some valuable study time. Skimming and scanning are reading techniques you should use when you study.

For example, do you reread the entire chapter the night before a test? Don't waste your study time doing that! Instead, use the skimming technique to review the chapter. Skimming has another practical academic use: If you find you didn't get the chapter read in time for class discussion, try previewing or overviewing as an emergency measure!

In Activity 7–2, you will learn about three specific techniques: previewing, overviewing, and reviewing. They will increase your ability to read only the parts that you need to know for a particular situation.

Begin by reading the selection entitled "Skimming and Scanning." On a separate sheet of paper, add to your notes on this topic. Then define the following new terms: *preview*; *review*; *overview*. Be sure to include examples of their uses.

Skimming and Scanning

You have already done a number of activities that focused on the skill of reading materials at different rates. Learning how to vary the rate at which you read is invaluable. It will not only save you time, it will increase your comprehension as well.

You have already been introduced to two types of very rapid reading:

Skimming: passing quickly over an entire selection to get a general idea or "gist" of its contents. For example, you skim a chapter in your history books to review your knowledge of the Civil War.

Scanning: glancing at a selection for a specific piece of information, and stopping when you find it. For example, you scan the *S* column in the telephone book looking for Joe Santiago's number.

The major difference, then, between skimming and scanning is that when you finish skimming, you have covered the entire selection briefly; in scanning, you glance only until you find what you are looking for, and then you stop.

Skimming and scanning both involve reading selectively. In other words, you read only those parts that will serve your purpose. Skimming, however, involves three basic forms of selective reading: previewing, overviewing, and reviewing.

Previewing: The prefix *pre* means before; to preview is to view the material *before* you actually begin reading it. Previewing is usually followed by a more thorough reading. You can use previewing to select a book, survey a chapter, or search for appropriate research material.

Overviewing: Overviewing is getting a "big picture" view of the material. Overviewing usually is *not* followed by another reading. You use overviewing to get an overall sense of the content of an article or book.

Reviewing: The prefix *re* means *again*. When you review, you view the material again. Reviewing follows a previous reading. You can use reviewing to go back over material to refresh your memory, especially before a test or important discussion.

Skimming and scanning are both done rapidly. Remember, though, they differ in purpose and length.

Activity 7–3
Your Personal Reading Rates

Now that you understand about flexible rates and varying purposes for reading, you will have an opportunity to see just how greatly your reading rates can vary. Intellectually, you know that you don't read everything at the same speed. As you follow the instructions for the reading rate samples, you will see just how different the rates really are.

You will begin by examining and recording your *slow and careful* rate—the rate you use when you study or when you want to remember specific details. Next, you will have an opportunity to use and record your *average* rate. This rate is used when you want to recall main ideas. A faster rate may be used when you are reading for pleasure. Recording your skimming speed will tell you how fast your *rapid* or "once over lightly" rate is. Your scanning rate will be *very rapid*, since you race along looking for a specific item when you scan. As you compare the different speeds, you will realize how variable your reading rates actually are.

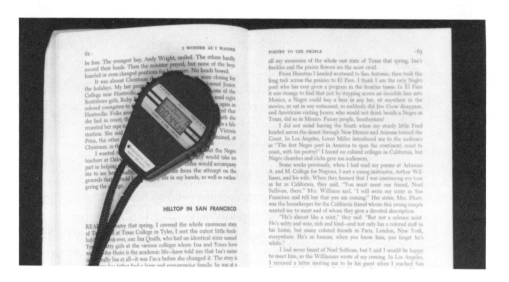

Activity 7–3
Reading Rate Chart

You will need a chart for recording your reading rates. Divide a sheet of paper into two columns. Label the columns with the headings shown in the illustration. Be sure to leave plenty of room to record times and answer questions. You will use this chart for Activities 7–4 through 7–8.

First, you will record the time you begin reading; then the time you stop reading. Then answer the comprehension questions.

After you have answered the questions, subtract the time you began from the time you stopped to find your total reading time.

Example: Time stopped   2:30

Time began   2:22

Total time   :08

Next, turn to page 120 to find the number of words per minute you read.

READING RATE CHART

Time	Minutes	Seconds
Activity 7–4 Slow and Careful		
Time stopped	_____	_____
Time began	_____	_____
Total time read	_____	_____
Words per minute	_____	
Score	_____	
Activity 7–5 Average		
Time stopped	_____	_____
Time began	_____	_____
Total time read	_____	_____
Words per minute	_____	
Score	_____	
Activity 7–6 Rapid		
Time stopped	_____	_____
Time began	_____	_____
Total time read	_____	_____
Words per minute	_____	
Gist of article:		
Activity 7–7 Very Rapid		
Time stopped	_____	_____
Time began	_____	_____
Total time read	_____	_____
Words per minute	_____	
What does it mean to "learn your boss's management style"?		

Activity 7–4
Slow and Careful Reading Rate

Before you begin reading the article, "Creating Successful Study Habits," note the time and write it on your paper. (For greater accuracy, if your instructor is not timing you, use a watch or clock with a second hand.)

Read this article at a *slow* and *careful* rate for maximum comprehension, because the material you will be reading is similar to that in a textbook, and you will be given a test over specific details from the article.

When you finish reading, again note and record the time. In order to compute the total amount of time you spent in reading the selection, subtract the time you began reading from the time you stopped.

Next, consult the conversion chart on page 120 in order to record your reading rate in words per minute.

To measure your comprehension, without looking back at the article, answer on a separate sheet of paper the ten true–false questions in the Comprehension Test section. Check your answers; then compute your score by multiplying by ten your number correct.

Creating Successful Study Habits

Webster's Dictionary states that a habit is something done often and easily. The word *often* should be emphasized whenever speaking about developing study habits. The habits that will help you be most successful in your studies are the ones that you repeat daily both at school and at home.

You should practice the following study habits daily:

Use an assignment sheet in every class;

Write down all assignments in full detail;

Read the assignment sheets after the end of your last class, but *before* leaving school;

Bring home all the books, worksheets, folders, and notebooks needed to complete the homework.

If you want to study and complete assignments successfully at home, you must develop these study habits *at school*. After all, the most common excuses for not finishing or doing homework are that the book was left at school or that the assignment was forgotten. You won't forget if you develop the study habits that help you remember these important items.

The study habits that will help you at home include the following:

Begin your homework at the same time every night;

Do your work in the same place each night;

Ask your parents or guardians to help you maintain a positive work environment.

Once again, you must repeat this routine every night in order to make these successful study habits. Common homework hassles such as difficulty getting started or failing to allow enough time to finish the work are avoided by starting the work at the same time each night. Your starting time should allow at least one and one-half hours for completing the assigned work.

Where you do your work should also become a habit. Always doing the work at the same location breeds success in several ways. First, it helps you to get started on your work at the same time each evening. Supplies you use often, such as paper, pen, pencil, ruler, and eraser, can all be stored at or near your study area. Thus, you avoid a time-consuming and distracting hunt for these items each night.

Your work area should be well lit and should include a large flat surface. It should also be as free of noisy distractions as possible. The most common distractions are televisions, radios, stereos, ringing telephones, and younger brothers and sisters. Every distraction makes it harder to complete the work and do it well.

In addition, the encouragement and support of a parent or guardian constitutes an important aspect of creating good study habits. Ask a parent to get in the routine of not only asking if you have homework, but also asking to see your day's assignment sheet. Your parent might help by quizzing you, or by assisting with any problems you encounter with an assignment. He or she might also review your completed work.

You'll finish your homework more quickly and efficiently if you adopt and practice the study habits discussed here. With self-discipline and dedication, you, too, can be a good student.

Below are ten questions. Read each one carefully. Then, on a separate sheet of paper, write the correct answer beside the appropriate number. **Do not** turn back to the article. When you finish, check your answers and multiply by ten your number correct. Record your comprehension score on your paper.

1. You should use an assignment sheet in:

   A. every class.   B. some classes.   C. important classes.

2. You should use the assignment sheet:

   A. often.   B. daily.   C. occasionally.

3. You should read the assignment sheet:

   A. at the end of each class period.

   B. after your last class ends, but before you leave school.

   C. before you start your homework at night.

4. Beginning homework at the same time each night:

   A. helps you get started more easily.

   B. provides you with enough time to finish everything.

   C. both of the above

5. Your starting time should allow you:

   A. a half hour of study time each night.

   B. one hour of study time each night.

   C. one and one-half hours of study time each night.

6. Doing your work in the same place each night:

   A. helps you get started at the same time each night.

   B. avoids delays because all your supplies are there.

   C. both of the above

7. According to the author, distractions should be avoided because:

   A. they slow you down.

   B. they make it harder for you to complete the work and do it well.

   C. both of the above

8. A parent might help by:

   A. asking if you have assignments.

   B. asking to see your assignment sheet.

   C. both of the above

9. A parent can also help by:

   A. quizzing you on your work.

   B. reviewing your completed work.

   C. both of the above

10. You will benefit from the study habits discussed in this article if you practice them:

   A. the evening before a test.

   B. at least three evenings each week.

   C. every evening.

Activity 7–5
Average Reading Rate

Let's go on to consider average reading and to determine your rate in words per minute. You will be using a light, entertaining selection that you can read at a faster rate than the previous article. However, do not read so fast that you lose comprehension.

Note the time and write it on your paper. Then begin reading. When you finish reading, again note the time and record it. Subtract the time you began from the time you stopped to determine the total time read. Turn to the Conversion Chart on page 120 to compute your words read per minute, and record this figure. Then take the comprehension test for this story.

Mary Had a Little Lamb

It's a little-known fact of nature that sharks are not the only animals which have feeding frenzies. The slightest hint of a milk bottle will send orphan (bum) lambs wild. They will stampede, trampling any hapless bystanders in the dust. Anyone brave enough to try feeding two bottles to more than two lambs will have fingers chewed, ears nibbled, and noses bitten. The mere presence of a known food supplier will turn a field of angelic bum lambs into a frenzied mob. Yet, there are some compensations to owning bums if you can solve the feeding problem. Pincushion is an example.

Pincushion and his sister Giraffe entered the world on a chilly, blustery March day. Preemies, they were too weak to stand, too small to have reached their mother if they could have stood. Only my timely arrival saved them from being put out of their misery by my husband, Chris, who thought they would never survive. I took them home to see if I could save them, while my husband gave the grieving ewe a new lamb who needed a mother.

Giraffe we named immediately. She had a long delicate face and looked for all the world like a miniature giraffe. Pincushion's name came later.

Once home I began the process of warming the half-frozen lambs. They were immersed in comfortably hot water and fed a small amount of brandy to warm their insides. After they were briskly rubbed dry, I gently forced colostrum milk down their throats with a needleless syringe. They were too weak to suck from a bottle.

Within two hours they could raise their heads and were placed in their new home—our bathtub with a rug in the bottom. Within four hours they had developed pneumonia, and the fight for their lives began. They were each given three shots—two antibiotics and a stimulant. Feeding continued every three to four hours. Shots were administered daily.

By the third day we seemed to have conquered the pneumonia. It looked as though we were going to save them. Then scours (diarrhea) hit them. The needles came out again. More medicine was administered, and Pincushion earned his name. None of our other bums had ever been given this many shots in this few days.

When the crisis passed, the lambs gained enough strength to stand and take faltering steps. We cheered their progress around the house. They began to suck a bottle of milk and rapidly became family pets.

These lambs weighed perhaps a pound apiece when they were born. Their legs resembled matchsticks. Their heads were as fine as a fawn's, and their emaciated bodies were painful to see. By the time they were two weeks old, their bodies had begun to fill out. My husband wanted his tub back. It was time to move the lambs to our lamb nursery.

In an old house we owned, we had set up a straw-lined pen for newborn bums. Pincushion and Giraffe were installed in this pen. Tragically, Giraffe's delicate constitution could not withstand the transition. Soon we were fighting a losing battle with pneumonia.

While Giraffe struggled to keep a spark of life, Pincushion grabbed hold of life. His small size allowed him to slip through the sides of his pen. Once outside he mingled with lambs six to ten times his size. Mealtimes were trample time for Pincushion. He was always on the bottom of the pile but always fighting his way toward the top.

Time and time again we placed him back in the nursery, plugging more holes each time. Time and time again we picked him up from the bottom of the heap when we returned to feed the bums. Finally, we left him with his new friends.

When Pincushion was about a month old we put a self-feeder in with the lambs. We were tired of having our fingers gnawed at feeding time. As soon as we saw that the bums had the hang of things, we left to complete our other chores. When we returned, Pincushion lay on the floor moaning and writhing in agony. His belly was distended to three times its normal size. He was a victim of his own gluttony.

With tears in my eyes I moved Pincushion back to his old bathtub to die in peace. I closed the shower curtains and left him there while I went to town for an appointment. I knew of nothing I could do to ease his agony, and I could not stand to see the end.

When I returned and threw back the shower curtains, Pincushion was gone. "Well," I thought, "he died, and Chris has taken the body away." Some need to say "good-bye" drove me to search the trash can—no Pincushion. "Chris probably took him somewhere so that I didn't have to see him"—my thoughts were interrupted by a faint bleating. I hurried to a small outdoor pen, and there Pincushion stood demanding to be fed.

The rest of the story I heard from Chris. He had stopped at the house to pick up the body a few hours after I left. He was sure that the lamb would have died by then. Instead he was greeted at the door by a

vigorous Pincushion, wanting food. He replaced Pincushion in the tub and closed the curtains, but before he could leave the bathroom, Pincushion was out of the tub and at his heels. That is when Pincushion was transferred to the outdoor pen.

When Pincushion could be trusted to digest all he could eat at the self-feeder, we transferred him back to the bum pen. Although the tiniest of all the lambs, once he grabbed a nipple at the feeder no lamb could ever dislodge him. He sucked until the last drop of milk was gone, oblivious of the other lambs who pushed, shoved, crawled over and under him. He thrived, grew, and finally became the leader of the bums.

Pincushion outgrew many of the bums and lived a long, pleasant summer with us. We never lacked for companionship when Pincushion was near. He followed at our heels, nudged us to be petted, and nuzzled us with affection.

We sold Pincushion in the fall. There is no room on a modern farm for a nonproducing animal. We turned our heads and could not look at this gentle friend and companion. We were ashamed that scarce dollars dictated the fate of Pincushion.

In his short time with us, he was a model of bravery, indomitable courage, perseverance and friendship. Tucked away with all my memories of good and fine things is the memory of Pincushion.

To measure your comprehension, without looking back at the article, answer the following ten questions. On a separate sheet of paper, write the letter of the correct answer beside the appropriate number. When you finish, check your answers and multiply by ten your number correct. Record your comprehension score on your paper.

1. A bum lamb is a lamb that is:

    A. deformed.   B. sick.   C. an orphan.

2. The sight of _____ will send angelic lambs into a frenzied mob.

    A. their mother.   B. a milk bottle.   C. hay.

3. Pincushion and Giraffe were sick because they were:

    A. cold.   B. preemies.   C. ignored.

4. In order to save the lambs, the author:

    A. immersed them in comfortably hot water and rubbed them dry.

    B. fed them a small amount of brandy and colostrum milk.

    C. both A and B

5. The first new home for the two lambs was:

    A. a bathtub.   B. a playpen.   C. an old house.

6. The lambs had to battle:

    A. pneumonia.   B. scours.   C. both A and B

7. The lamb that showed the greatest will to survive was:

    A. Pincushion.   B. Giraffe.   C. neither A nor B

8. Pincushion battled for survival a fourth time because of:

    A. the cold.   B. greed for food.   C. the other lambs.

9. Pincushion survived because of:

    A. loving care.   B. a strong spirit.   C. both A and B

10. The author:

    A. cared very much for the lambs.

    B. was happy to sell the lambs and take a profit.

    C. wondered why she spent so much time with the lambs.

Activity 7–6
Rapid Reading Rate

The next reading rate we will focus on is skimming. There is a technique to skimming efficiently. Try it on the article entitled "Figure Out What the Boss Wants":

    A. Read the title.

    B. Read the introduction (first four paragraphs).

    C. Read the ten rules (headings only).

    D. Read the conclusion (last two paragraphs).

Begin by noting the time and writing it on your chart. Then skim "Guidelines for Succeeding with Your Boss," using the method outlined above.

When you finish, record the time you stopped; then subtract the time you began from the time you stopped to determine the total time read. Turn to the Conversion Chart on page 120 to compute your words read per minute.

Next, to check your comprehension, write a brief paragraph explaining the gist of the article.

Guidelines for Succeeding with Your Boss

All the books and articles on how to make good at work usually ignore one very basic premise in "how to get ahead." This practical bit of wisdom never seems to come up in polite conversation, although every employee from the office assistant to the vice-president is well aware of it.

Figure Out What the Boss Wants

There is no mystery to this; it is really only common sense. Find out how your boss likes to be dealt with and learn how to do it. You will both benefit.

Here are ten guidelines for getting along with your boss that surveyors of management methods have gleaned from their work with bosses of all types.

    1. *Be professional.* Bosses set the tone for the degree of formality or informality that they are most comfortable with in the workplace. Also, as a general rule, to avoid embarrassment for one or both of you, personal problems are usually best left at home.

2. *Respect them and their authority.* Remember that the buck stops with them. They are ultimately responsible for every success or failure. Don't challenge their right to tell you what to do or to judge what you have done. They are paid to do just that. It is their job.

3. *They are in touch with the whole picture.* You deal with only one aspect of the company's business. Their scope of responsibility is much greater than yours. They may, in turn, report to several bosses instead of one, as you do.

4. *Is your timing appropriate?* At what time of the day is your boss most receptive to new ideas? When is he or she most likely to be irritable? Be aware of your boss's schedule. Think about what might be happening in the company that will demand his or her undivided attention. Then plan your time with your boss accordingly.

5. *Learn their management style.* Some bosses delegate a lot of authority. Others do not. Some bosses expect to be consulted about everything. Others expect you to do your job on your own, once you have instructions. Some bosses are very formal in their manner, while others are more relaxed and friendly. Learn all you can about your boss's style.

6. *Find out how they prefer to be contacted.* Can you drop by anytime, or do you need an appointment? Can you do your business over the phone, or does your boss prefer that you sit down across the desk from him or her?

7. *They are only human.* Many people expect their bosses to be perfect and then complain when they are not. Remember, bosses make mistakes and say things without thinking just as you do. They also may have other things on their minds when you approach them. Recognize that they, too, are human, and you will avoid much anxiety and misunderstanding when some days do not go as smoothly as you would like.

8. *Keep them aware of what goes on.* This is the highest priority for many bosses surveyed. They want to know who, what, why, when, and where. They need to know these "five Ws" in order to plan ahead, make decisions, and report to their own bosses. When you are reporting to them about something, be sure to learn whether they like to know all the details or want only general information. Also remember that bosses like to learn the good news as well as the bad. It may be a pleasant change.

9. *Don't try too hard to please the boss.* To constantly try to please makes you less than a favorite among your co-workers, and you

For success on the job, learn your boss's management style.

probably spend more time with them than with your boss, anyway. There's an old saying that "cream always rises to the top." Your path will be smoother if, on the way up, you get along with others.

10. *Bosses are individuals.* Keep this in mind when trying to understand them. They are not a company—they are real and unique people. Management techniques are helpful only if they relate to your particular boss.

You will benefit by learning about your bosses' management styles. Of course, the best way to succeed with your boss is to do your job well, but the extra effort it takes to learn more about his or her style of operating pays dividends for both of you.

Remember, if you look good, your boss looks good. Your ability to help your boss do his or her job better will lead you to even more success in the future.

Activity 7–7
Very Rapid Reading Rate

To conclude this survey of your reading rates, focus now on scanning, the fastest reading rate of all. Note the time you begin and write it on your chart; then turn back to page 117 and scan the article "Guidelines for Succeeding with Your Boss" to answer this question: What does it mean to "learn your boss's management style"?

As you finish, record the time you stopped; subtract your starting time from your stopping time and convert the result to words per minute using the chart on page 120. Answer the question briefly.

Now take a look at the range of your personal reading rates. You may read at speeds of 100 to 200 words per minute or at speeds approaching or exceeding 1,000 words per minute. Whatever your rates, no doubt you'll agree: Your reading rate is flexible.

Activity 7–8
Conversion Chart for Reading Rates

COMPUTING READING RATES IN WORDS PER MINUTE

Slow and Careful

"Creating Successful Study Habits"

550 words total

2 minutes = 276 words per minute
2:10 = 254 words per minute
2:20 = 236 words per minute
2:30 = 219 words per minute
2:40 = 206 words per minute
2:50 = 194 words per minute
3:00 = 183 words per minute
3:10 = 174 words per minute
3:20 = 165 words per minute
3:30 = 157 words per minute
3:40 = 150 words per minute
3:50 = 144 words per minute
4:00 = 138 words per minute
4:10 = 132 words per minute
4:20 = 127 words per minute
4:30 = 122 words per minute
4:40 = 118 words per minute
4:50 = 114 words per minute
5:00 = 110 words per minute

Average

"Mary Had a Little Lamb"

1,120 words total

3 minutes = 373 words per minute

3:10 = 358 words per minute   5:10 = 218 words per minute
3:20 = 343 words per minute   5:20 = 212 words per minute
3:30 = 328 words per minute   5:30 = 206 words per minute
3:40 = 313 words per minute   5:40 = 200 words per minute
3:50 = 298 words per minute   5:50 = 194 words per minute
4:00 = 280 words per minute   6:00 = 186 words per minute
4:10 = 271 words per minute   6:10 = 182 words per minute
4:20 = 262 words per minute   6:20 = 178 words per minute
4:30 = 253 words per minute   6:30 = 174 words per minute
4:40 = 244 words per minute   6:40 = 170 words per minute
4:50 = 235 words per minute   6:50 = 166 words per minute
5:00 = 224 words per minute   7:00 = 160 words per minute

Rapid Skimming

"Guidelines for Succeeding with Your Boss"

692 words total

:30 seconds = 1,384 words per minute
:40 seconds = 1,038 words per minute
:50 seconds =   830 words per minute
1:00 minute =   692 words per minute
1:10 minutes =   593 words per minute
1:20 minutes =   519 words per minute
1:30 minutes =   461 words per minute
1:40 minutes =   415 words per minute
1:50 minutes =   377 words per minute

Very Rapid Scanning

"Guidelines for Succeeding with Your Boss"

:10 seconds = 2,400 words per minute
:20 seconds = 1,200 words per minute
:30 seconds =   800 words per minute
:40 seconds =   600 words per minute
:50 seconds =   480 words per minute
1:00 minute =   400 words per minute
1:10 minutes =   343 words per minute
1:20 minutes =   300 words per minute
1:30 minutes =   266 words per minute

Activity 7–9
Skimming a Book

Any skills that save you time and make you a better reader are skills worth learning. Skimming and scanning will do just that. Try the following exercise using skimming to improve your rapid reading techniques.

Periodically, you will need to select a book for a project, report, or research paper, and you will have to look at several books before choosing the best one for the assignment. Knowing how to skim a book quickly will be a valuable skill.

To give you practice in skimming for this purpose, select a book that pertains to a research assignment you have currently. Or, choose a book from those provided for you by your instructor. Then use the following technique to skim it:

1. Look at the title, author, and publication date. Has the book been reprinted? If so, how many times? Is the publication date recent enough to be appropriate for your research topic?

2. Read the publisher's comments on the cover or dust jacket;

3. Look at the preface or other introductory material;

4. Look at the Table of Contents (if there is one);

5. Look at the first chapter, using a skimming (previewing) technique;

6. Leaf through the rest of the book, looking at major headings, charts, pictures, graphs, and so on.

Now, on a separate sheet of paper, write a brief paragraph summarizing the contents of the book and conclude with a statement of whether the book will be of value to you.

Activities 7–10, 7–11, 7–12, and 7–13
More Skimming and Scanning

The next four activities will give you practice in scanning. The activities are similar to those you might do in everyday situations at school or at work. Without scanning, these would become very time-consuming tasks. Imagine how long it would take to use the dictionary, telephone book, or encyclopedia if you had to start at the beginning and look at every entry until you came to the information you were seeking. Clearly, scanning is an essential reading technique.

Use a separate sheet of paper and a watch or clock with a second hand to time yourself if your instructor is not timing you. Be sure to note and record the time you begin and the time you finish each exercise. When you finish, subtract the time you started from the time you finished to compute the total time it took you to do the exercise.

Next, check your answers for accuracy and write a brief sentence explaining why this was an exercise in scanning. Can you see improvement as you compare your reading rates and the accuracy you achieved?

In Activity 7–11, play close attention to the column headings at the top of the flight schedule and to the symbols and abbreviations at the bottom of the schedule. Your speed is not as important in this activity as your accuracy. You will use this type of information if you plan a trip for yourself or plan trips professionally for others.

TWA

From:

ALBUQUERQUE, N.M. (ABQ)

Reservations:
Passenger: 243-8611
Getaway Tours: 800-523-4828
Español: 800-421-8261
Freight: 505-842-4157

Freq.	Leave	Arrive	Flt. No.	Stops/ Meal
To: ATHENS, Greece (ATH) (H)				
	8 10a	11 00a†	742/880	C M
	10 00a	11 00a†	94/844/880	C M
To: BALTIMORE, Md. (BWI)				
	10 00a	5 11p	94/228	C S
To: BARCELONA, Spain (BCN)				
	8 10a	10 20a†	742/900	C M
	10 00a	10 20a†	94/844/900	C M
To: BOSTON, Mass. (BOS)				
	8 10a	3 27p	742/310	C M
	10 00a	5 37p	94/752	C S
	12 55p	8 30p	408/206	C M
To: CAIRO, Egypt (CAI) (H)				
X17	8 10a	3 20p†	742/840	C M
17	8 10a	4 35p†	742/840	C M
X17	10 00a	3 20p†	94/844/840	C M
17	10 00a	4 35p†	94/844/840	C M
To: CHICAGO, Ill. (ORD) (H)				
	8 10a	11 40a	742	0 M
	10 00a	2 49p	94/810	C S
	12 55p	5 50p	408/296	C M
To: CINCINNATI, Ohio (CVG)				
	10 00a	4 04p	94/56	C S
X6	12 55p	7 11p	408/456	C M
X6	3 40p	9 41p	526/444	C S
To: CLEVELAND, Ohio (CLE)				
	10 00a	4 25p	94/292	C S
X6	3 40p	10 13p	526	1 S
To: COLUMBUS, Ohio (CMH)				
	10 00a	4 21p	94/598	C S
	12 55p	7 17p	408/124	C M
X6	3 40p	10 02p	526/100	C S
To: DAYTON, Ohio (DAY)				
	10 00a	4 10p	94/500	C S
To: DETROIT, Mich. (DTW)				
	10 00a	4 23p	94/590	C S
	2 45p	9 56p	490	2 S
X6	3 40p	9 56p	526/490	C S
To: FRANKFURT, Germany (FRA) (H)				
	8 10a	8 05a†	742/740	C M
	8 10a	10 30a†	742%	2 M
	10 00a	8 05a†	94/844/740	C M
To: HARRISBURG, Pa. (MDT)				
	10 00a	4 42p	94/396	C S
To: HARTFORD, Conn./ SPRINGFIELD, Mass. (BDL)				
	10 00a	8 02p	94/118	C M
To: INDIANAPOLIS, Ind. (IND)				
	10 00a	3 01p	94/136	C S
	12 55p	6 13p	408/184	C M
X6	3 40p	8 29p	526/446	C S
To: KANSAS CITY, Mo. (MCI)				
	12 55p	3 39p	408	0 M
To: LAS VEGAS, Nev. (LAS)				
	4 30p	9 17p	103/705	C
To: LISBON, Portugal (LIS)				
	8 10a	6 40a†	742/900	C M
	10 00a	6 40a†	94/844/900	C M
To: LITTLE ROCK, Ark. (LIT)				
	12 55p	6 13p	408/491	C M
To: LONDON, England (LHR/LGW) (H) AIRPORTS: G-Gatwick H-Heathrow				
	8 10a	H 6 45a†	742/700	C M
	8 10a	G 7 15a†	742/706	C M
	10 00a	H 6 45a†	94/844/700	C M
	10 00a	G 7 15a†	94/844/706	C M
	10 00a	H 7 25a†	94/752/754	C M
X126	10 00a	H 7 45a†	94/708	C M
	12 55p	H 9 05a†	408/296/770	C M
X236	12 55p	H 9 40a†	408/158/756	C M
	3 16p	H 12 00n†	453/760	C M
To: LOS ANGELES (LAX)/ ONTARIO, Cal. (ONT) AIRPORTS: L-Los Angeles				
	8 30a	L 9 18a	231	0 M
	3 16p	L 4 06p	453	0 S
	6 05p	L 6 55p	237	0 M
To: LOUISVILLE, Ky. (SDF)				
	10 00a	4 12p	94/406	C S
X6	3 40p	9 30p	526/434	C S
To: MADRID, Spain (MAD)				
	8 10a	8 40a†	742/904	C M
	10 00a	8 40a†	94/844/904	C M
To: MIAMI, Fla. (MIA)				
	10 00a	8 59p	94/492	C M
To: MILAN, Italy (MXP) (H)				
	8 10a	9 35a†	742/842	C M
	10 00a	9 35a†	94/844/842	C M
To: NASHVILLE, Tenn. (BNA)				
	10 00a	2 59p	94/372	C S
6	2 45p	8 38p	490/516	C S
X6	3 40p	8 38p	526/518	C S
To: NEW YORK, N.Y. (JFK/LGA)/ (H) [helicopter] NEWARK, N.J. (EWR) AIRPORTS: L-LaGuardia J-Kennedy E-Newark				
X6	8 10a	E 3 17p	742/464	C M
	8 10a	L 3 24p	742/320	C M
	8 10a	J 4 17p	742	1 M
	10 00a	J 5 19p	94/844	C S
	10 00a	L 5 24p	94/250	C S
	10 00a	E 5 36p	94/274	C S
X6	12 55p	L 8 40p	408	1 M
X6	3 40p	L 10 50p	526/460	C S
To: PALM SPRINGS, Cal. (PSP)				
	4 30p	8 55p	103/235	C
To: PARIS, France (CDG) (H)				
	8 10a	8 35a†	742/800	C M
	10 00a	8 35a†	94/844/800	C M
	10 00a	9 30a†	94/810	C M
	12 55p	9 30a†	408/206/810	C M
To: PEORIA, Ill. (PIA)				
X6	3 40p	8 41p	526/495	C S
To: PHILADELPHIA, Pa. (PHL)				
	10 00a	5 16p	94/482	C S
X6	12 55p	8 26p	408/158	C M
X6	3 40p	10 54p	526/558	C S
To: PHOENIX, Ariz. (PHX)				
X7	7 00a	7 03a	101	0
	4 30p	4 35p	103	0
To: PITTSBURGH, Pa. (PIT)				
	10 00a	6 02p	94/598/22	C S
	10 00a	6 55p	94/108	C S
X6	12 55p	8 35p	408/456	C M
X6	3 40p	10 16p	526/242	C M
To: ROME, Italy (FCO) (H)				
	8 10a	8 50a†	742/840	C M
X17	10 00a	8 30a†	94/752/846	C M
	10 00a	8 50a†	94/844/840	C M
17	10 00a	10 05a†	94/844	C M
X17	10 00a	11 05a†	94/844	C M
To: ST. LOUIS, Mo. (STL)				
	10 00a	1 12p	94	0 S
	2 45p	6 51p	490	1 S
X6	3 40p	6 55p	526	0 S
To: SAN DIEGO, Cal. (SAN)				
	6 05p	9 41p	237/65	C M
To: SAN FRANCISCO (SFO)/ SAN JOSE, Cal. (SJC) AIRPORTS: S-San Francisco J-San Jose				
	4 30p	S 6 55p	103	1 S
	4 30p	J 9 05p	103/63	C S
To: SAN JOSE, Cal. (SJC)				
	4 30p	J 9 05p	103/63	C S
To: SYRACUSE, N.Y. (SYR)				
	10 00a	7 42p	94/564	C M
To: TAMPA/ST. PETERSBURG/ CLEARWATER, Fla. (TPA)				
	10 00a	7 36p	94/492	C M
To: TEL AVIV, Israel (TLV) (H)				
	8 10a	3 50p†	742/806	C M
	10 00a	3 50p†	94/810/806	C M
	10 00a	3 50p†	94/844/806	C M
To: TUCSON, Ariz. (TUS)				
	4 30p	8 39p	103/371	C
To: WASHINGTON, D.C. (DCA/IAD)/ BALTIMORE, Md. (BWI) AIRPORTS: N-National D-Dulles I-Baltimore-Washington				
	8 10a	N 2 59p	742/204	C M
X6	10 00a	N 4 30p	94/708	C S
	10 00a	N 5 00p	94	1 S
	10 00a	I 5 11p	94/228	C S
	12 55p	N 7 46p	408/230	C M
To: WICHITA, Kan. (ICT)				
	2 45p	5 08p	490	0

From:

AMARILLO, Texas (AMA)

Reservations:
Passenger: 376-4880
Getaway Tours: 800-523-4828
Español: 800-421-8261
Freight: 335-1665

Freq.	Leave	Arrive	Flt. No.	Stops/ Meal
To: BOSTON, Mass. (BOS)				
	1 55p	8 30p	296/206	C M
To: CHICAGO, Ill. (ORD) (H)				
	1 55p	5 50p	296	2
To: CINCINNATI, Ohio (CVG)				
X6	1 55p	7 11p	296/456	C
To: COLUMBUS, Ohio (CMH)				
	1 55p	7 17p	296/124	C S
To: DETROIT, Mich. (DTW)				
	1 55p	9 56p	296/490	C S
To: INDIANAPOLIS, Ind. (IND)				
	1 55p	6 13p	296/184	C
To: KANSAS CITY, Mo. (MCI)				
	1 55p	4 02p	296	1
To: LITTLE ROCK, Ark. (LIT)				
	1 55p	6 13p	296/491	C
To: LONDON, England (LHR/LGW) (H) AIRPORTS: G-Gatwick H-Heathrow				
	1 55p	H 9 05a†	296/770	C M
To: LOS ANGELES (LAX)/ ONTARIO, Cal. (ONT) AIRPORTS: L-Los Angeles				
	8 40a	L 10 00a	297	1 M
To: NASHVILLE, Tenn. (BNA)				
X6	1 55p	8 38p	296/518	C
To: NEW YORK, N.Y. (JFK/LGA)/ (H) [helicopter] NEWARK, N.J. (EWR) AIRPORTS: L-LaGuardia J-Kennedy E-Newark				
X6	1 55p	L 8 40p	296/408	C M
To: PARIS, France (CDG) (H)				
	1 55p	9 30a†	296/206/810	C M
To: PHILADELPHIA, Pa. (PHL)				
X6	1 55p	8 26p	296/158	C M
To: PHOENIX, Ariz. (PHX)				
	8 40a	8 15a	297	0 M
To: PITTSBURGH, Pa. (PIT)				
X6	1 55p	8 35p	296/456	C
To: ST. LOUIS, Mo. (STL)				
	1 55p	6 51p	296/490	C S
To: SAN FRANCISCO (SFO)/ SAN JOSE, Cal. (SJC) AIRPORTS: S-San Francisco J-San Jose				
	8 40a	S 1 33p	297/111	C M
To: WASHINGTON, D.C. (DCA/IAD)/ BALTIMORE, Md. (BWI) AIRPORTS: N-National D-Dulles I-Baltimore-Washington				
	1 55p	N 7 46p	296/230	C M
To: WICHITA, Kan. (ICT)				
	1 55p	2 48p	296	0

From:

ATHENS, Greece (ATH) (H)

Reservations:
Passenger: 3226451
Freight: 9702211

Freq.	Leave	Arrive	Flt. No.	Stops/ Meal
To: BOSTON, Mass. (BOS)				
X123	10 50a	3 45p	847	1 M
3	10 50a	3 45p	847%	1 M
To: CAIRO, Egypt (CAI) (H)				
X12	2 25p	3 20p	840	0 S
12	3 40p	4 35p	840	0 S
To: CHICAGO, Ill. (ORD) (H)				
X12	10 50a	6 18p	841/847/811	C M
	1 00p	8 45p	881/743	C M
To: CINCINNATI, Ohio (CVG)				
	1 00p	7 46p	881/423	C M
To: CLEVELAND, Ohio (CLE)				
	1 00p	9 12p	881/219	C M
To: COLUMBUS, Ohio (CMH)				
	1 00p	8 46p	881/573	C M
To: DALLAS/ FT. WORTH, Texas (DFW)				
	1 00p	9 00p	881/901	C M
To: DAYTON, Ohio (DAY)				
	1 00p	8 58p	881/703	C M
To: DENVER, Colo. (DEN)				
	1 00p	9 20p	881/211	C M
To: DETROIT, Mich. (DTW)				
	1 00p	9 22p	881/701	C M
To: HOUSTON, Texas (IAH)				
	1 00p	9 03p	881/801	C M
To: INDIANAPOLIS, Ind. (IND)				
	1 00p	7 53p	881/423	C M
To: KANSAS CITY, Mo. (MCI)				
	1 00p	11 02p	881/743	C M
To: LOS ANGELES (LAX)/ ONTARIO, Cal. (ONT) AIRPORTS: L-Los Angeles				
X12	10 50a	L 7 59p	841/847/65	C M
	10 50a	L 9 14p	841%	2 M
	1 00p	L 9 14p	881/841	C M
To: MIAMI, Fla. (MIA)				
	1 00p	9 33p	881/5	C M
To: NEW ORLEANS, La. (MSY)				
	1 00p	8 03p	881%	1 M
To: NEW YORK, N.Y. (JFK/LGA)/ (H) [helicopter] NEWARK, N.J. (EWR) AIRPORTS: L-LaGuardia J-Kennedy E-Newark				
	10 50a	J 4 40p	841	1 M
	1 00p	J 4 25p	881	0 M
To: PHILADELPHIA, Pa. (PHL)				
	1 00p	7 01p	881/573	C M
To: PHOENIX, Ariz. (PHX)				
	1 00p	11 37p	881/167/579	C M
To: PITTSBURGH, Pa. (PIT)				
	1 00p	8 55p	881/167	C M
To: ROME, Italy (FCO) (H)				
	10 50a	11 45a	841	0 S
To: ST. LOUIS, Mo. (STL)				
	1 00p	9 16p	881/423	C M
To: SAN ANTONIO, Tx. (SAT)				
	1 00p	9 57p	881%	2 M
To: SAN DIEGO, Cal. (SAN)				
X12	10 50a	9 41p	841/847/65	C M
To: SAN FRANCISCO (SFO)/ SAN JOSE, Cal. (SJC) AIRPORTS: S-San Francisco J-San Jose				
X12	10 50a	S 9 31p	847%	2 M
	1 00p	S 9 14p	881/843	C M
To: WASHINGTON, D.C. (DCA/IAD)/ BALTIMORE, Md. (BWI) AIRPORTS: N-National D-Dulles I-Baltimore-Washington				
	1 00p	N 7 06p	881/703	C M

From:

BALTIMORE, Md. (BWI)

Reservations:
Passenger: 301-338-1155
Getaway Tours: 800-523-1027
Español: 800-421-8261
Freight: 301-859-2525

Freq.	Leave	Arrive	Flt. No.	Stops/ Meal
To: ALBUQUERQUE, N.M. (ABQ)				
X6	10 10a	1 34p	393	1 M
X6	3 55p	7 49p	511/477	C M
To: DENVER, Colo. (DEN)				
	10 10a	1 30p	393/561	C M
X6	3 55p	7 44p	511/753	C M
To: DES MOINES, Iowa (DSM)				
	10 10a	1 21p	393/271	C S
X6	3 55p	7 41p	511/519	C
To: HOUSTON, Texas (IAH)				
	10 10a	2 05p	393/221	C M
X6	3 55p	8 14p	511/597	C M
To: KANSAS CITY, Mo. (MCI)				
	10 10a	12 41p	393/485	C S
X6	3 55p	6 54p	511/557	C
To: LAS VEGAS, Nev. (LAS)				
	10 10a	1 59p	393/419	C M
X6	3 55p	8 00p	511/521	C M
To: LITTLE ROCK, Ark. (LIT)				
	10 10a	1 18p	393/309	C S
X6	3 55p	7 47p	511/771	C
To: LOS ANGELES (LAX)/ ONTARIO, Cal. (ONT) AIRPORTS: L-Los Angeles				
	10 10a	L 1 52p	393/91	C M
X6	3 55p	L 8 22p	511/269	C M
To: OKLAHOMA CITY, Okla. (OKC)				
	10 10a	1 24p	393/567	C S
X6	3 55p	7 54p	511	1 S
To: OMAHA, Neb. (OMA)				
	10 10a	1 13p	393/243	C S
X6	3 55p	7 43p	511/559	C S

TIME
Effective July 1, 1982

Schedules Shown in Local Time

SYMBOLS
% Plane Change Enroute
† Arrival One Day Later

[helicopter] New York Helicopter JFK-LGA-EWR-NYC

C Connecting Flight
* Change of Airport

M Meal
S Snack

(H) Hilton International
★ Night Coach Fares Apply

PAGE 3

Activity 7–10

Number a separate sheet of paper from one to fifteen, note and record the time, and begin. Arrange the following list of dates in order, starting with the least recent and ending with the most recent.

10/5/75	4/25/85	8-08-80
June 1, 1966	August 12, 1970	1/12/83
6-21-76	Nov. 4, 1980	2/14/84
January 25, 1979	12-25-84	March 17, 1977
May 1, 1982	7-02-72	September 5, 1981

Did you use skimming or scanning to do this exercise?

Activity 7–11

Write your responses to the following on a separate sheet of paper. Use the flight schedule provided to answer the questions.

1. If you were going from Albuquerque, New Mexico, to Chicago, Illinois, how many flights would you have to choose from?

2. If you wanted to go from Albuquerque to Chicago and arrive before noon, when would you leave Albuquerque?

3. What is the number of the flight described in Question 2 above?

4. On the flight described in Question 2 above, would you be served a meal or a snack?

5. If you wanted to book a flight out of Amarillo, Texas, what telephone number would you call for reservations?

6. If you went from Amarillo to Nashville, when would you leave Amarillo?

7. What time would you arrive in Nashville?

8. What is the number of the flight described in Question 6 above leaving Amarillo?

9. What is the number of the flight you would connect (C) with before you reached Nashville?

10. If you wanted to go from Athens, Greece, to Denver, Colorado, what time would you leave Athens?

11. What time would you arrive in Denver?

12. Is there a connecting flight between Athens and Denver, or is it a non-stop flight?

13. What is the abbreviation used for Denver, Colorado?

14. If you were going from Athens to New York/Newark, New Jersey, how many airports are listed that you could fly to?

15. Of these airports, which is the only one TWA serves?

16. Of the two flights listed leaving Athens and arriving in New York, what is the number of the flight that takes the least amount of travel time?

17. If you were going from Albuquerque, New Mexico, to Athens, Greece, on the 10:00 A.M. flight, how many connecting flights would you have to make?

18. When would the flight arrive in Athens?

19. If you were going from Albuquerque, New Mexico, to Cleveland, Ohio, on the 3:40 P.M. flight, how many stops would you make?

Activities 7–12 and 7–13

Skimming, to review, is reading through an entire selection quickly to get a general idea of its content. Many students find skimming to be one of the most useful techniques they have learned; we hope it will be valuable to you, also.

Besides saving you lots of time, skimming improves your comprehension, as well. In fact, skimming followed by actual reading can double comprehension. Try it, and you'll soon see the value of skimming.

How much information can you get by just skimming something? You will get an opportunity to compare test scores on information you skim with test scores on information you read completely. Both tests will use the same material.

Remember, when you master skimming, you will be able to preview, review, or overview material quickly and easily. Think just how invaluable this technique is for both school and work situations.

In order to skim efficiently, use the following method:

1. Read the title of the selection;

2. Read the first paragraph;

3. Read the first sentence of each of the other paragraphs;

4. Read the final paragraph.

Use a separate sheet of paper. Label it as shown below:

Skimming		Actual Reading	
Time stopped	_____	Time stopped	_____
Time began	_____	Time began	_____
Total time	_____	Total time	_____
Words per minute	_____	Words per minute	_____
Score	_____	Score	_____

Activity 7–12: Skimming

If your instructor is not timing you, use a watch or a clock with a second hand to note the times you start and finish each exercise. Record these times on your paper. When you are ready, or when your instructor gives the signal, begin reading "Cycling's Risks" using the skimming technique described previously in Steps 1 to 4. When you finish with the exercise, subtract the time you started from the time you stopped to determine the total time used. Then turn to the Conversion Chart (page 129) to figure the number of words per minute. Next, number a separate sheet of paper from one to ten and answer the Comprehension Test questions.

Activity 7–13: Actual Reading

Now read the entire article entitled "Cycling's Risks." Record the times you begin and finish. Subtract your beginning time from your finishing time to find total time read; again, turn to the Conversion Chart on page 129 to convert the results to words per minute. Take the Comprehension Test again, writing your answers on a separate sheet of paper. Also, now that you have read all of the article, make any changes you want to in your answers to the first Comprehension Test you took after using skimming.

For *each* test (after skimming and then after actual reading) multiply your number correct by ten to get your percentage scores. Record these scores in the appropriate blanks. Now compare them. How many answers did you change? (If you scored 70 percent or better on the skimming test, you are using skimming very effectively.) Notice how much information you got simply by skimming. Did you notice skimming helping you to improve your comprehension when you did the actual reading of the article? You will find that you can use skimming to your benefit with many kinds of reading materials.

Cycling's Risks

My noncycling friends think bike racers are crazy. They can't believe how long road races are. If they get on a bike and try to sustain 20 m.p.h. they become exhausted. As a result they are flatly incredulous when I tell them that races go at 25 to 28 m.p.h. for several hours. Sprinters' hills loom like mountains in their minds and the Mt. Evans Hill Climb is simply unimaginable. When I assert that the training which brings such performances within reach is enjoyable rather than agonizing, they nod knowingly to one another.

But these doubters reserve their most vehement attacks on my sanity for what they perceive as the unacceptable dangers of cycling. Recently a friend picked up an old copy of a racing publication and read about Alan Kingsbery's near-fatal collision with a truck crossing a time trial course. When he finished he looked at me searchingly. "How can you justify your sport," he asked, "when you have a wife and son?"

I did not consider the question idle, presumptuous or even rhetorical. I have asked it of myself at times, especially after crashes or close calls.

Certainly there are safer activities for a person in his thirties who has heavy responsibilities in life. But because I enjoy cycling so much, I find it easy to justify—what dangers there are seem eminently worth the risk. Yet part of me realizes that my justifications are not the real reason I ride in spite of the hazards. Consider how easily I can find excuses to ignore the danger:

Given the state of automobile accident statistics, I am probably at least as safe when racing, commuting and training as I would be in a car.

Wearing a hardshell cycling helmet cuts down on the risk of serious injury and fatality. And I wear one at all times, not just when racing.

We have to take some calculated risks in life. Man is by nature a risk-taker, a challenger of limits, or he would not have evolved. In fact, the whole evolutionary history of life is a history of the risks that nature takes when minute individual differences are introduced into the species. Many of these fail, but some are successful and lead to improved adaptation to the challenges of life. In the same way, an individual human life without risk would result in a stagnant personality. Thoreau was right: When it comes time for me to die, I do not want to look back on my life and find that I have not lived.

Racing helps me to stay fit. The alternative, a sedentary lifestyle, is more deadly than any danger faced while cycling. Of course, I could get fit by swimming, but I have no talent for it—I would probably drown (that really is an unjustifiable risk). Serious running, for me, is unhealthy. My knees can rarely handle runs over twenty miles and my hips get sore at random, apparently just to be contrary. Although it may be argued that I could maintain my fitness by recreational cycling and avoid the sport's dangers, I see commuting, training and racing as part of the whole experience. Each reinforces and gives meaning to the others until the composite attitude toward transportation, health, enjoyment and competition merges into a lifestyle.

I am safer in cycling than in other sports I could choose. I played football enthusiastically and with abandon for ten years, but the major injury and death statistics from that sport continue to appall me. After college I got involved in mountaineering. I still have recurring visions of a basketball-size boulder bounding at me down a couloir on Crestone Needle. It missed; my knees shook for an hour. When I downhill ski it is either me or the mountain and I've never won yet. I could become a motorcycle racer, a cliff diver, a Pipeline surfer or an Indy driver. In comparison to many sports, not to mention wars or everyday household accidents, cycling is outrageously safe.

Even though all these arguments roll glibly off my tongue, responsibility to family remains a disturbing and pertinent point. However, I would rather take a small and calculated risk to be a fit, alive, interesting

and exuberant cyclist than come ponderously home each evening to the TV and snack tray. The risks of such a lifestyle may be less obvious than those of racing, but they are more insidious, more deadly and, to my mind, far less acceptable. In the end I can easily justify my cycling: We cannot choose the time and manner of our deaths, but we can have a say in the style and quality of our lives.

But to list reasons why I can accept the dangers of cycling is merely to eliminate the negative. Trying to justify cycling by checking off the debits ignores the positive reasons for racing and training that overwhelm the drawbacks.

My reasons for racing do not arise out of a simplistic view of competition. I rarely taste the thrill of victory; as for the agony of defeat, I try to keep my performances in proper perspective. Racing is certainly not my whole life nor do I wish it to be. When I am honest with myself I realize that I race for three reasons, all compelling, but none noble or unselfish.

I race because I hate pain. I know that such an admission, besides sounding like a paradox, is inconsistent with the cliché of the macho cyclist picking gravel out of grisly abrasions while gritting his teeth on a spare crankset bolt, but it is true. The longer I have been involved in sports, the more fascinated I have been by my reaction to pain. I have become addicted to the process of facing that pain and trying to beat my fear and loathing. The result is now a post-race euphoria that is only slowly replaced by accelerating anxiety about the next contest. Aristotle may not have been a bike racer, but he knew about fear and pain. He called it catharsis: a combination of pity, terror and relief. He was

talking about the audience's reaction to tragedy, but it is applicable to us moderns as we experience self-inflicted "sports-pain"—pity for ourselves at the specter of approaching pain, terror that it will hurt so much we'll quit or slow down and get dropped, and finally relief that the demon has been met face to face and conquered, or at least confronted honestly. In the weekly cycle of quiescence, anxiety, competition and catharsis, my fear and hatred of pain is purged.

I also race because I like to ride with other people—sometimes. Since I live far from the area where most of Colorado's races and riders are located, I usually train alone. I prefer it that way because I can ride when it fits my schedule. But part of the thrill of cycling is how bikes handle around other bikes: the vacuum, suction, lightening sensation of a big pack, the psychedelic patterns of alloys and jerseys, the sense of shared enterprise and momentary alliances, the way the pack develops a mind and will of its own, independent of, and yet connected to, each rider's perceptions and personality. Nowhere is this better experienced than in a race where individuals merge into one sinuous group while still maintaining their separate wills and motivations and personalities. When I train alone I clear my head of all the trivia of the day. But when I am in a pack of riders I feel a part of the race sharing the hopes, dreams and honest fears of everyone else.

Finally, I simply like to ride a bicycle and racing gives me an excuse to do it often. I don't need to justify my riding to other people, but when daily tasks press hard on the time I set aside for me, it helps to be able to justify it to myself.

On a separate sheet of paper, write *true* if the statement is true and *false* if the statement is false.

1. Noncyclists think bike racers are to be admired for their bravery.

2. Noncyclists think cycling is dangerous.

3. Fred Matheny, the author of this article, feels he is as safe when cycle racing as when riding in a car.

4. Matheny feels wearing a helmet offers very little protection from *serious* injury.

5. The author believes in taking risks to some degree.

6. He feels he is safer in cycling than in playing football or in downhill skiing, but not as safe as when swimming.

7. Matheny prefers to ride with others all the time.

8. Matheny uses racing as an excuse to ride his bike simply because he loves to ride it.

9. The author periodically considers giving up bicycle racing because of the dangers involved and because he hates pain.

10. Matheny thinks about bike racing's dangers versus his responsibility to his family.

CONVERSION CHART: SKIMMING AND ACTUAL READING

"Cycling's Risks"

1,110 words total

30 sec = 2,200 words per minute		3:50 min = 287 words per minute
40 sec = 1,666 words per minute		4:00 min = 275 words per minute
50 sec = 1,325 words per minute		4:10 min = 264 words per minute
1:00 min = 1,110 words per minute		4:20 min = 254 words per minute
1:10 min = 943 words per minute		4:30 min = 244 words per minute
1:20 min = 827 words per minute		4:40 min = 236 words per minute
1:30 min = 733 words per minute		4:50 min = 227 words per minute
1:40 min = 662 words per minute		5:00 min = 220 words per minute
1:50 min = 601 words per minute		5:10 min = 212 words per minute
2:00 min = 550 words per minute		5:20 min = 206 words per minute
2:10 min = 507 words per minute		5:30 min = 200 words per minute
2:20 min = 472 words per minute		5:40 min = 194 words per minute
2:30 min = 440 words per minute		5:50 min = 188 words per minute
2:40 min = 413 words per minute		6:00 min = 183 words per minute
2:50 min = 388 words per minute		6:10 min = 179 words per minute
3:00 min = 366 words per minute		6:20 min = 175 words per minute
3:10 min = 347 words per minute		6:30 min = 171 words per minute
3:20 min = 330 words per minute		6:40 min = 167 words per minute
3:30 min = 314 words per minute		6:50 min = 163 words per minute
3:40 min = 300 words per minute		7:00 min = 159 words per minute

Activity 7–14
Unit Review

On a separate sheet of paper, number from one to twenty-five. Follow the directions for each section of the review and write your answers beside the corresponding numbers on your answer sheet.

I. Vocabulary Terms
    Use the following terms to identify the type of reading described below:

skimming   preview   very rapid reading   slow and careful reading

scanning   review   rapid reading   average reading

overview

1. This follows a previous reading and is used when you go back over material to study for a test or to prepare a report.

2. Moving quickly over an entire selection to get the gist of it is _____.

3. This is most often followed by a second reading; it is used in selecting a book, surveying a chapter before reading it, and so on.

4. This rate is used when covering difficult concepts and vocabulary, when reading technical material, and when it's necessary to retain every detail.

5. This rate is used for light, easy, and entertaining reading.

6. When you glance over material very quickly until you find a desired piece of information, and then you stop reading, you are using _____.

7. A reading to get a general impression of the material is a(n) _____; it is not followed by another reading.

8. This rate is used for magazine articles, some chapters in social studies, and so on, and is about 250 words per minute.

9. This rate is for fairly easy material and when you want only the more important facts.

II. Completion
     Write the correct answer in the corresponding space on your answer sheet.
     10 to 12. Your reading rate is determined by three factors. They are
                ____10____, ____11____, and ____12____.

     13 to 14. Two other factors that influence *your own ability* to read rapidly
                are ____13____ and ____14____.

     15 to 18. The four steps in skimming an essay, a chapter, or a book are
                ____15____, ____16____, ____17____, and ____18____.

III. Application

The following are descriptions of material you might encounter and the purposes you might have for reading it. Read the description and the purpose. Then select the appropriate reading rate from the list provided. Write the rate you have chosen beside the corresponding number on your answer sheet.

scanning   very rapid   average
skimming   rapid   slow and careful

	Type of Material	Your Purpose	Rate
19.	The chapter in a social studies textbook on Reconstruction after the Civil War	You need to understand completely. A test on details is coming up.	?
20.	A light, fast-moving Louis L'Amour story, *Buck, the Cowboy Renegade*	You are reading for pleasure.	?
21.	An encyclopedia article on the life of Herbert Hoover	You want to know what college President Hoover attended.	?
22.	Your English teacher has made the following assignment: List the characteristics of a good writer.	You need to research several articles to locate the parts that list the characteristics. You will read them more carefully later.	?
23.	An interesting adventure story in a magazine	You are reading in the dentist's waiting room to pass the time.	?
24.	You bought a new car. You are considering what type of insurance to buy.	You want to understand fully the extent of the coverage you need.	?
25.	Local news in your paper	You want to know what's going on in your town.	?

Using the Dictionary

USING (yōōz' ing) v. to put into service

DICTIONARY (dĭk' shə-nĕr' ē) n. a reference book containing an alphabetical list of words and their meanings

ictionaries contain a lot of information. You may know that a dictionary can help you spell and find the meanings of unfamiliar words. But what you may not know is that a dictionary can also help you find words that have similar meanings, give you the population of Mankato, Minnesota, and tell you when the expression "last straw" was first used to refer to something other than the one that broke the camel's back. Information that you may have felt you needed to use an encyclopedia to find might instead be found in your dictionary.

Knowing how to use a dictionary is a valuable study skill. Once you learn how to find the information you need quickly, you can improve both your reading and writing skills.

Activity 8–1
Alphabetical Order

Not all dictionaries are alike. The dictionary you use at school may be different from the one you use at home or in the library. But one thing all dictionaries have in common is their basic organization; words are arranged in alphabetical order. So, to find a word in a dictionary—*any* dictionary—you need to know the order of letters in the alphabet.

Why should you improve your alphabetizing skills? Alphabetizing skills are especially useful when you are using a dictionary; however, they are also helpful when you want to find a section in the Sunday paper, locate a book in a library card catalog, or find a file in an office drawer.

Follow the instructions for each step of Activity 8–1. Try to increase your speed as you work through each section.

Section One

Using a separate sheet of paper, number from one to ten. Next to the corresponding number write the letters that come right before and right after the letter that is shown. For instance, in the first example using the letter *w*, *v* comes before *w* in the alphabet, and *x* comes after *w*.

1. __v__ w __x__   6. ____ s ____
2. ____ b ____   7. ____ g ____
3. ____ x ____   8. ____ c ____
4. ____ m ____   9. ____ l ____
5. ____ j ____   10. ____ q ____

Section Two

Using a separate sheet of paper, number from one to twelve. This time supply the missing letter in each group of letters. The first has been done as an example.

1. b __c__ d   7. w ____ y
2. v ____ x   8. e ____ g
3. j ____ l   9. t ____ v
4. q ____ s   10. m ____ o
5. a ____ c   11. f ____ h
6. i ____ k   12. g ____ i

Dictionaries are valuable tools for building reading and writing skills.

Section Three

Using a separate sheet of paper, number from one to ten. In the groups of letters below, the letters are scrambled. Write the one letter that should come *first* in each group beside the example.

1. b   f   g   (a)   6. l   f   s   k
2. m   p   z   l   7. t   s   r   x
3. r   x   c   g   8. l   p   d   q
4. q   s   v   y   9. h   e   k   i
5. w   t   m   p   10. i   m   k   q

Activity 8–2
Alphabetical Order

Using a separate sheet of paper, number from one to ten. Write the words in each group below as they would appear in alphabetical order. Note that each set of words begins with the same letter. You will have to look to the second or third letter to arrange these words. Use the first set as an example.

1. easy
   easement
   east

   Answer:
   easement, east, easy

2. grand
   garage
   garbage

3. locomotive
   locomotion
   location

4. shield
   shelter
   sheet

5. clank
   clangor
   clang

6. twilight
   twinkle
   twist

7. wood
   waste
   wonder

8. indent
   incident
   indicator

9. atomic
   atrocious
   attach

10. upstairs
    upstart
    upstage

Activity 8–3
Dictionary Terms and Definitions

Most people think of a dictionary only as a source of word meanings or spellings. Activity 8–3 gives you an opportunity to find other kinds of information in each dictionary entry. For example, do you know where the inflected form of a word is found? Or its variant spelling? What about the word's etymology? Are these all new terms to you?

The following illustration shows where in a typical dictionary entry to find such information. Remember that a page from your own dictionary may look slightly different from the page shown here; just check the beginning of your version for a section explaining how your dictionary is organized.

In the following illustration you'll notice various vocabulary terms—each serving as a label to identify some part of a dictionary entry. As you read on, you'll learn more about the meaning of these vocabulary terms and how your knowing and using them can sharpen your study skills.

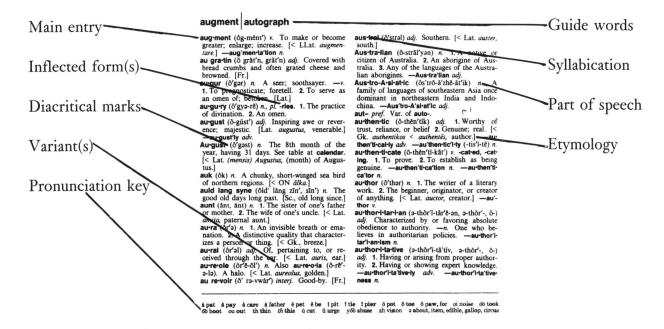

Main entry · Inflected form(s) · Diacritical marks · Variant(s) · Pronunciation key · Guide words · Syllabication · Part of speech · Etymology

On a separate sheet of paper, take notes on the following dictionary terms and their definitions. Keep your notes brief.

Main Entry

The *main entry* is the word or phrase that you look up. It is usually printed in bold type in a position slightly to the left of the body of the entry.

Syllabication

The *syllabication* shows how a word is divided. The divisions are usually indicated by small dots. You can use syllabication when you write to determine how to divide a word at the end of a line. **Example:** goal • keep • er.

When you have to divide a word at the end of a line, you should follow the syllabication shown in your dictionary. However, also keep in mind these three rules:

1. Do not divide one-syllable words (house);

2. Do not divide a word so that only one letter is left on a line (able); and

3. Try to divide hyphenated words only at the hyphen (self-control).

Variants

Variants are two or more correct spellings of a single word. They are usually in bold type and may be treated in two ways:

1. If a variant spelling is separated from the main entry by the word *or* (or a comma in some dictionaries), that variant spelling is used as frequently as the spelling of the main entry. **Example:** *ax or axe (ax, axe).* Both spellings, *ax* and *axe,* are used equally frequently.

2. If a variant spelling is separated from the main entry by *also*, the main entry spelling is preferred. **Example:** *medieval* also *mediaeval. Medieval* is the preferred spelling.

Etymology

A word's *etymology* indicates its origin (where it came from) and the etymological meaning of the word in that language. Etymologies usually appear in brackets or in parentheses. **Example:** the origin of the word retract is [< Lat. *retractare,* to handle again]. Etymologies may come directly after the main entry or, as in the sample dictionary page shown, at the end of the dictionary entry. A question mark in the etymology means that the origin of the word is unknown.

Inflected Forms

Inflections are changes in the form of a word due to a tense change or a plural form. To save space, dictionaries list only irregular inflected forms, such as the plural *oxen* for *ox* or the past tenses *swam* and *swum.* (If *ox* was regular, its plural would be *oxs,* and it would not be listed in the dictionary; if *swim* was regular, its past tense would be *swimmed,* and it would not be listed.)

Inflected forms usually appear in bold type following the label specifying part of speech. If inflected forms are not listed for a word, you can assume that these forms are regular.

You may want to look up inflected forms when you need to know any of the following information: the plural form of a word or how to spell it, or the past tense of a word or how to spell it. **Example:** *think* v. *thought, thinking.*

Parts of Speech

A word's *part of speech* is usually indicated by italic type (letters that slant) and often follows the main entry. It is important to check a word's part of speech to make sure that you do not use a word incorrectly. For example, when you see in the dictionary that a particular word is a noun, you won't try to use it as a verb. The part of speech is usually abbreviated. Some common abbreviations include the following:

n. — noun	*pron.* — pronoun
v. — verb	*conj.* — conjunction
adj. — adjective	*interj.* — interjection
adv. — adverb	

Homographs

Homographs are words that have the same spelling, but different meanings and origins. **Example:** *bark*—the noise a dog makes; *bark*—the outer covering of a tree; *bark*—a three-masted sailing ship.

Diacritical Marks

Diacritical marks are the dots, dashes, and other signs that show how to pronounce a word. The system for using these signs is usually explained in a *Pronunciation Key* at the top or bottom of the page. **Example:** potato (pə-tā′tō).

Guide Words

Guide words are the words at the top of the dictionary page. The guide words indicate the first and last main entry words found on that page. They help you to locate more quickly the word you want. **Example: broadcast / broth.**

Activity 8–4
Recognizing Dictionary Components

On a separate sheet of paper, number from one to nine. Use the following illustration to identify the numbered components of the dictionary entry. Choose the correct term from the list provided, and use each of the terms one time. Write the term beside the appropriate number on your paper.

main entry	pronunciation key	diacritical marks
etymology	part of speech	syllabication
guide words	variant	inflected forms

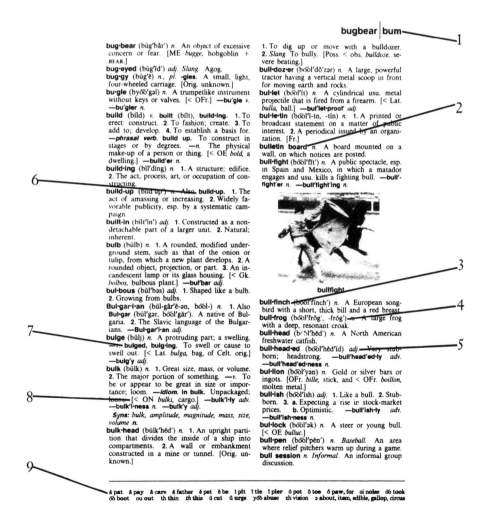

bugbear | bum ——1

bug·bear (bŭg′bâr′) *n.* An object of excessive concern or fear. [ME *bugge*, hobgoblin + BEAR.]
bug-eyed (bŭg′īd′) *adj. Slang.* Agog.
bug·gy (bŭg′ē) *n., pl.* **-gies.** A small, light, four-wheeled carriage. [Orig. unknown.]
bu·gle (byōō′gəl) *n.* A trumpetlike instrument without keys or valves. [< OFr.] **—bu′gle** *v.* **—bu′gler** *n.*
build (bĭld) *v.* **built, build·ing. 1.** To erect; construct. **2.** To fashion; create. **3.** To add to; develop. **4.** To establish a basis for. **—phrasal verb. build up.** To construct in stages or by degrees. **—n.** The physical make-up of a person or thing. [< OE *bold*, a dwelling.] **—build′er** *n.*
build·ing (bĭl′dĭng) *n.* **1.** A structure; edifice. **2.** The act, process, art, or occupation of constructing.
build-up (bĭld′ŭp′) *n.* Also. **build-up. 1.** The act of amassing or increasing. **2.** Widely favorable publicity, esp. by a systematic campaign.
built-in (bĭlt′ĭn′) *adj.* **1.** Constructed as a nondetachable part of a larger unit. **2.** Natural; inherent.
bulb (bŭlb) *n.* **1.** A rounded, modified underground stem, such as that of the onion or tulip, from which a new plant develops. **2.** A rounded object, projection, or part. **3.** An incandescent lamp or its glass housing. [< Gk. *bolbos*, bulbous plant.] **—bul′bar** *adj.*
bul·bous (bŭl′bəs) *adj.* **1.** Shaped like a bulb. **2.** Growing from bulbs.
Bul·gar·i·an (bŭl-gâr′ē-ən, bōōl-) *n.* **1.** Also **Bul·gar** (bŭl′gər, bōōl′gär′). A native of Bulgaria. **2.** The Slavic language of the Bulgarians. **—Bul·gar′i·an** *adj.*
bulge (bŭlj) *n.* A protruding part; a swelling. **—v. bulged, bulg·ing.** To swell or cause to swell out. [< Lat. *bulga*, bag, of Celt. orig.] **—bulg′y** *adj.*
bulk (bŭlk) *n.* **1.** Great size, mass, or volume. **2.** The major portion of something. **—v.** To be or appear to be great in size or importance; loom. **—idiom. in bulk.** Unpackaged; loose. [< ON *bulki*, cargo.] **—bulk′i·ly** *adv.* **—bulk′i·ness** *n.* **—bulk′y** *adj.*
Syns: bulk, amplitude, magnitude, mass, size, volume **n.**
bulk·head (bŭlk′hĕd′) *n.* **1.** An upright partition that divides the inside of a ship into compartments. **2.** A wall or embankment constructed in a mine or tunnel. [Orig. unknown.]

1. To dig up or move with a bulldozer. **2.** *Slang.* To bully. [Poss. < obs. *bulldose*, severe beating.]
bull·doz·er (bōōl′dō′zər) *n.* A large, powerful tractor having a vertical metal scoop in front for moving earth and rocks.
bul·let (bōōl′ĭt) *n.* A cylindrical usu. metal projectile that is fired from a firearm. [< Lat. *bulla*, ball.] **—bul′let-proof** *adj.*
bul·le·tin (bōōl′ĭ-tn, -tĭn) *n.* **1.** A printed or broadcast statement on a matter of public interest. **2.** A periodical issued by an organization. [Fr.]
bulletin board *n.* A board mounted on a wall, on which notices are posted.
bull·fight (bōōl′fīt′) *n.* A public spectacle, esp. in Spain and Mexico, in which a matador engages and usu. kills a fighting bull. **—bull′fight·er** *n.* **—bull′fight·ing** *n.*

bullfight

bull·finch (bōōl′fĭnch′) *n.* A European songbird with a short, thick bill and a red breast.
bull·frog (bōōl′frôg′, -frŏg′) *n.* A large frog with a deep, resonant croak.
bull·head (bōōl′hĕd′) *n.* A North American freshwater catfish.
bull·head·ed (bōōl′hĕd′ĭd) *adj.* Very stubborn; headstrong. **—bull′head′ed·ly** *adv.* **—bull′head′ed·ness** *n.*
bul·lion (bōōl′yən) *n.* Gold or silver bars or ingots. [OFr. *bille*, stick, and < OFr. *boillon*, molten metal.]
bull·ish (bōōl′ĭsh) *adj.* **1.** Like a bull. **2.** Stubborn. **3. a.** Expecting a rise in stock-market prices. **b.** Optimistic. **—bull′ish·ly** *adv.* **—bull′ish·ness** *n.*
bul·lock (bōōl′ək) *n.* A steer or young bull. [< OE *bulluc*.]
bull·pen (bōōl′pĕn′) *n. Baseball.* An area where relief pitchers warm up during a game.
bull session *n. Informal.* An informal group discussion.

——2

——3

——4

——5

——6

——7

——8

——9

ă pat ā pay â care ä father ĕ pet ē be ĭ pit ī tie î pier ŏ pot ō toe ô paw, for oi noise ōō took
ōō boot ou out th thin *th* this ŭ cut û urge yōō abuse zh vision ə about, item, edible, gallop, circus

Activity 8–5
Discovering Etymologies

English is a language that has borrowed words and phrases from many languages. Sometimes the etymology of a word can help you determine its meaning, as when the word comes from a common Latin or Greek root. Other times, the meaning of the word has changed so much that it has little relation to the foreign word it developed from. For these reasons, discovering a word's etymology and etymological meaning can be very interesting.

The following activity will give you practice in reading etymologies in dictionary entries. Be sure to follow the instructions for each step.

Begin by numbering a separate sheet of paper from one to seventeen. Using the dictionary entries provided, find the etymology for each of the words listed.

---

emporium | encumber

employing. **2.** The state of being employed. **3.** An activity or occupation.

em·po·ri·um (ĕm-pôr'ē-əm, -pōr'-) *n., pl.* **-ums** or **-po·ri·a** (-pôr'ē-ə, -pōr'-). A store carrying a wide variety of merchandise. [< Gk. *emporion*, market.]

em·pow·er (ĕm-pou'ər) *v.* To invest with legal power; authorize.

em·press (ĕm'prĭs) *n.* **1.** The female sovereign of an empire. **2.** The wife or widow of an emperor. [< OFr. *emperesse.*]

emp·ty (ĕmp'tē) *adj.* **-ti·er, -ti·est. 1.** Containing nothing. **2.** Having no occupants or inhabitants; unoccupied. **3.** Lacking purpose, substance, value, or effect. —*v.* **-tied, -ty·ing. 1.** To make or become empty. **2.** To discharge or flow: *a river that empties into a bay.* —*n., pl.* **-ties.** An empty container, esp. a bottle. [< OE *æmtig.*] —**emp'ti·ness** *n.*

emp·ty-hand·ed (ĕmp'tē-hăn'dĭd) *adj.* **1.** Bearing nothing in the hands. **2.** Having gained or accomplished nothing.

em·py·re·an (ĕm'pī-rē'ən) *n.* **1.** The highest reaches of heaven. **2.** The sky or firmament. [< Gk. *empurios,* fiery.]

e·mu (ē'myōō) *n.* A large, flightless Australian bird related to and resembling the ostrich. [Port. *ema,* flightless bird of South America.]

em·u·late (ĕm'yə-lāt') *v.* **-lat·ed, -lat·ing.** To strive to equal or excel, esp. through imitation. [Lat. *aemulari.*] —**em'u·la'tion** *n.*

e·mul·si·fy (ĭ-mŭl'sə-fī') *v.* **-fied, -fy·ing.** To make into or become an emulsion. —**e·mul'si·fi·ca'tion** *n.* —**e·mul'si·fi'er** *n.*

e·mul·sion (ĭ-mŭl'shən) *n.* **1.** A suspension of small globules of one liquid in a second liquid with which the first does not mix. **2.** A light-sensitive coating, usu. of silver halide grains in a thin gelatin layer, on photographic film, paper, or glass. [< Lat. *emulgēre,* to drain out.] —**e·mul'sive** *adj.*

en (ĕn) *n. Printing.* A unit of measure equal to half the width of an em.

en-¹ or **em-** *pref.* **1. a.** To put into or on: *enthrone.* **b.** To go into or on: *entrain.* **2.** To cover or provide with: *enrobe.* **3.** To cause to be: *endear.* **4.** Thoroughly. Used often as an intensive: *entangle.* [< Lat. *in,* in.]

en-² or **em-** *pref.* In; into; within: *empathy.* [< Gk.]

-en¹ *suff.* **1. a.** To cause to be: *cheapen.* **b.** To become: *redden.* **2. a.** To cause to have: *hearten.* **b.** To come to have: *lengthen.* [< OE *-nian.*]

-en² *suff.* Made of or resembling: *wooden.* [< OE.]

en·a·ble (ĕn-ā'bəl) *v.* **-bled, -bling. 1.** To provide with the means, knowledge, or opportunity; make possible. **2.** To give legal power, capacity, or sanction to.

en·act (ĕn-ăkt') *v.* **1.** To make (a bill) into a law. **2.** To act out, as on a stage. —**en·act'ment** *n.*

e·nam·el (ĭ-năm'əl) *n.* **1.** A vitreous, usu. opaque coating baked on metal, glass, or ceramic ware. **2.** A paint that dries to a hard, glossy surface. **3.** The hard substance that covers the exposed portion of a tooth. —*v.* **-eled** or **-elled, -el·ing** or **-el·ling.** To coat or decorate with enamel. [< AN *enamailler,* to put on enamel.] —**e·nam'el·ware'** *n.*

en·am·or (ĭ-năm'ər) *v.* Also chiefly Brit. **en·am·our.** To inspire with love; captivate. [< OFr. *enamourer.*]

en bloc (äN blŏk') *adv.* All together; as a whole. [Fr.]

en·camp (ĕn-kămp') *v.* To set up or live in a camp. —**en·camp'ment** *n.*

en·cap·su·late (ĕn-kăp'sə-lāt') *v.* **-lat·ed, -lat·ing.** To encase or become encased in a capsule. —**en·cap'su·la'tion** *n.*

en·case (ĕn-kās') *v.* **-cased, -cas·ing.** To enclose in or as if in a case. —**en·case'ment** *n.*

-ence or **-ency** *suff.* Action, state, quality, or condition: *reference.* [< Lat. *-entia.*]

en·ceph·a·li·tis (ĕn-sĕf'ə-lī'tĭs) *n.* Inflammation of the brain. —**en·ceph'a·lit'ic** (-lĭt'ĭk) *adj.*

encephalo- or **encephal-** *pref.* The brain: *encephalitis.* [< Gk. *enkephalos,* in the head.]

en·ceph·a·lon (ĕn-sĕf'ə-lŏn') *n., pl.* **-la** (-lə). The brain of a vertebrate. [Gk. *enkephalon.*]

en·chain (ĕn-chān') *v.* To bind with or as if with chains; fetter.

en·chant (ĕn-chănt') *v.* **1.** To cast under a spell; bewitch. **2.** To delight completely; enrapture. [< Lat. *incantare.*] —**en·chant'er** *n.* —**en·chant'ment** *n.*

en·chi·la·da (ĕn'chə-lä'də) *n.* A rolled tortilla with a meat or cheese filling, served with a sauce spiced with chili. [Mex. Sp.]

en·ci·pher (ĕn-sī'fər) *v.* To put (a message) into cipher. —**en·ci'pher·ment** *n.*

en·cir·cle (ĕn-sûr'kəl) *v.* **-cled, -cling. 1.** To form a circle around; surround. **2.** To move or go around; make a circuit of. —**en·cir'cle·ment** *n.*

en·clave (ĕn'klāv', ŏn'-) *n.* A country or part of a country lying entirely within the boundaries of another. [< OFr. *enclaver,* to enclose.]

en·close (ĕn-klōz') *v.* **-closed, -clos·ing.** Also **in·close** (ĭn-). **1.** To surround on all sides; fence in. **2.** To include in the same container with a package or letter. [< Lat. *includere,* to include.] —**en·clo'sure** (-klō'zhər) *n.*

en·code (ĕn-kōd') *v.* **-cod·ed, -cod·ing.** To put (a message) into code. —**en·cod'er** *n.*

en·co·mi·um (ĕn-kō'mē-əm) *n., pl.* **-ums** or **-mi·a** (-mē-ə). Lofty praise; eulogy. [< Gk. *enkōmios,* of the victory procession.]

en·com·pass (ĕn-kŭm'pəs, -kŏm'-) *v.* **1.** To surround. **2.** To comprise or contain; include.

en·core (ŏn'kôr', -kōr') *n.* **1.** A demand by an audience for an additional performance. **2.** An additional performance in response to an audience's demand. —*v.* **-cored, -cor·ing.** To demand an encore of or from. [< Fr., again.]

en·coun·ter (ĕn-koun'tər) *n.* **1.** A casual or unexpected meeting. **2.** A hostile confrontation, as between enemies; clash. —*v.* **1.** To meet, esp. unexpectedly. **2.** To confront in battle. [< OFr. *encountre.*]

en·cour·age (ĕn-kûr'ĭj, -kŭr'-) *v.* **-aged, -ag·ing. 1.** To inspire with courage or confidence. **2.** To help bring about; foster. [< OFr. *encoragier.*] —**en·cour'age·ment** *n.* —**en·cour'ag·ing·ly** *adv.*

en·croach (ĕn-krōch') *v.* To intrude or infringe gradually upon the property or rights of another; trespass. [< OFr. *encrochier,* to seize.] —**en·croach'ment** *n.*

en·crust (ĕn-krŭst') *v.* Also **in·crust** (ĭn-). To cover or become covered with or as if with a crust. —**en'crust·a'tion** (ĕn'krŭ-stā'shən) *n.*

en·cum·ber (ĕn-kŭm'bər) *v.* **1.** To weigh down excessively; burden. **2.** To hinder; impede. [< OFr. *encombrer,* to block up.] —**en·cum'brance** (-brəns) *n.*

Write the etymology out in full (do not use abbreviations), and, if it is given, write the etymological meaning for each word. (Etymological meanings are found with the etymologies in the square brackets.)

You will need to know these abbreviations:

Gk—Greek	*Port*—Portuguese	*Fr*—French
OFr—Old French	*Lat*—Latin	*Mex Sp*—Mexican Spanish
OE—Old English	*AN*—Anglo-Norman	

1. enchilada
2. emporium
3. enclave
4. encroach
5. emu

6. enclose
7. encore
8. enamel
9. empty
10. encumber

11 to 17. Now write all the words from the dictionary page shown that have Old French as their etymology.

Activity 8–6
Using Other Information in a Dictionary Entry

This activity gives you practice in using some of the other information that is given in a dictionary entry. This time, you will check word division and find inflected forms of words. Why are these skills worth practicing? Because, in order to spell and write words correctly, you must know how they are divided and how their forms vary.

On a separate sheet of paper, number from one to ten. Refer to the dictionary entry provided as you answer the questions listed in Section One and Section Two below.

Section One: Syllabication

Using the dictionary entries on the next page, look up the words listed, determine their proper division into syllables, and write the syllabicated words beside the correct number on your paper.

1. glacial
2. gladiator
3. glamour

4. gladiolus
5. glaciate

gird (gûrd) *v.* gird·ed or girt (gûrt), gird·ing. 1. To encircle with or as if with a belt or band. 2. To fasten with a belt. 3. To equip or prepare for action. [< OE *gyrdan.*]
gird·er (gûr′dər) *n.* A strong horizontal beam used as a main support in building.
gir·dle (gûr′dl) *n.* 1. A belt, sash, or band worn around the waist. 2. A supporting undergarment worn over the waist and hips. —*v.* -dled, -dling. To encircle with or as if with a belt. [< OE *gyrdel.*] —gir′dler *n.*
girl (gûrl) *n.* 1. A female child or young unmarried woman. 2. *Informal.* A woman. 3. A sweetheart. 4. A female servant. [ME *girle.*] —girl′hood *n.* —girl′ish *adj.* —girl′ish·ly *adv.* —girl′ish·ness *n.*
girl Friday *n.* A female assistant with a great variety of duties.
girl·friend (gûrl′frĕnd′) *n.* Also girl friend. 1. A female friend. 2. *Informal.* A sweetheart or favored female companion of a man.
Girl Scout *n.* A member of the Girl Scouts, an organization for girls between 7 and 17 that stresses physical fitness, good character, and homemaking ability.
girt (gûrt) *v.* A *p.t.* & *p.p.* of gird.
girth (gûrth) *n.* 1. Size measured by encircling something; circumference. 2. A strap encircling an animal's body to secure a load or saddle. [< ON *györdh.*]
gist (jĭst) *n.* The central idea; essence. [< OFr., it lies.]
give (gĭv) *v.* gave (gāv), giv·en (gĭv′ən), giv·ing. 1. a. To make a present of: *give flowers.* b. To make gifts. c. To deliver in exchange or in recompense: *give five dollars for the book.* 2. To entrust to or place in the hands of: *Give me the scissors.* 3. To convey: *Give him my*

gla·cial (glā′shəl) *adj.* 1. Of, relating to, or derived from glaciers. 2. Often Glacial. Characterized or dominated by the existence of glaciers. 3. Extremely cold. [Lat. *glacialis,* icy.] —gla′cial·ly *adv.*
gla·ci·ate (glā′shē-āt′, -sē-) *v.* -at·ed, -at·ing. 1. To subject to glacial action. 2. To freeze. [Lat. *glaciare,* to freeze.] —gla·ci·a′tion *n.*
gla·cier (glā′shər) *n.* A large mass of slowly moving ice, formed from compacted snow. [< Lat. *glacies,* ice.]
glad (glăd) *adj.* glad·der, glad·dest. 1. Feeling, showing, or giving joy and pleasure; happy. 2. Pleased; willing: *glad to help.* [< OE *glæd.*] —glad′ly *adv.* —glad′ness *n.*
Syns: glad, cheerful, cheery, festive, gay, joyful, joyous *adj.*
glad·den (glăd′n) *v.* To make or become glad.
glade (glād) *n.* An open space in a forest. [Perh. < GLAD, shining (obs.)]
glad hand *n.* A hearty, effusive greeting. —glad′-hand′ *v.*
glad·i·a·tor (glăd′ē-ā′tər) *n.* 1. A man trained to entertain the public by engaging in fights to the death in ancient Roman arenas. 2. A person who engages in a sensational struggle. [Lat.] —glad′i·a·to′ri·al (-ə-tôr′ē-əl, -tōr′-) *adj.*
glad·i·o·lus (glăd′ē-ō′ləs) *n., pl.* -li (-lī′, -lē′) or -lus·es. A widely cultivated plant with sword-shaped leaves and a spike of showy, variously colored flowers. [< Lat. *gladius,* sword.]
glad·some (glăd′səm) *adj.* Glad; joyful. —glad′some·ly *adv.* —glad′some·ness *n.*
glam·or·ize (glăm′ə-rīz′) *v.* -ized, -iz·ing. Also glam·our·ize. To make glamorous. —glam′or·i·za′tion *n.* —glam′or·iz′er *n.*
glam·our (glăm′ər) *n.* Also glam·or. An air of

Section Two: Inflected Forms

Using the same group of dictionary entries (above), look up the following words and write their inflected forms beside the correct number on your answer sheet.

6. give

7. glaciate

8. glamorize

9. glad

10. gird

Activity 8–7
Using Diacritical Marks

You have come across a new word in your reading. Looking up the meaning of that new word is not enough to learn it. You must also know how to pronounce the word, so you can say it as well as write it. Diacritical marks help you learn a word's pronunciation. They are the focus of this activity.

Section One

On a separate sheet of paper, number from one to ten. Using the pronunciation key as a guide, determine the pronunciation of the words in the left-hand column. Then match the words with their correct definitions by placing the letter of the definition beside the corresponding number on your answer sheet.

1. glā′shər   A. to act out, as on a stage

2. ô-thĕn′tĭk   B. having dark or brown hair

3. o′thər   C. the writer of a literary work

4. ĕn-ăkt′   D. to inspire with courage

5. ĕn-klōz′   E. to surround on all sides

6. brōō-nĕt′   F. the forehead

7. brou   G. genuine, real

8. ĕn-kûr′ĭj   H. the central idea

9. jĭst   I. the eighth month of the year

10. ô-gəst′   J. a large mass of slowly moving ice

Section Two

The joke written below belongs to the "oldies but goodies" category. Use the dictionary pronunciation key to decipher it. Then, on a separate sheet of paper, write the answers to the questions that follow it.

Door′ing ə foot′bol gam, wun uv thə pla′ərs had ə kup′əl uv fing′gərs bad′le smash′d. Thə tem dok′tər igzamin′d and dres′d thə hand.

"Dok′tər," ask′d thə pla′ər angk′shəs-le, "wil i be abəl too pla thə pe-an′o?"

"Surtn′le yoo wil," promis′d thə dok′tər.

"Yoo′r wun′dər-fəl, dok′tər," sed thə hap′e plaər. "I kood nev′ər pla thə pe-an′o bi-for′!"

1. What happened to the football player?

2. What did the doctor promise him?

3. Why was the football player so pleased?

Activity 8–8
Other Kinds of Information in a Dictionary

Besides information about words and their meanings, many dictionaries provide information about geographical places and famous people. In addition, some dictionaries give information about grammar, punctuation, correct form for writing letters, and how to footnote information. Dictionaries may also include illustrations, so you can see what different alphabets look like or how a disc brake is constructed.

Morse code table:

A	·—		V	···—
B	—···		W	·——
C	—·—·		X	—··—
D	—··		Y	—·——
E	·		Z	——··
F	··—·		Ä	·—·—
G	——·		É	··—··
H	····		Ñ	——·——
I	··		Ö	———·
J	·———		Ü	··——
K	—·—		1	·————
L	·—··		2	··———
M	——		3	···——
N	—·		4	····—
O	———		5	·····
P	·——·		6	—····
Q	——·—		7	——···
R	·—·		8	———··
S	···		9	————·
T	—		0	—————
U	··—			

, (comma)   ——··——
. (period)   ·—·—·—
?   ··——··
:   ———···
;   —·—·—·
/   —··—·
- (hyphen)   —····—
apostrophe   ·————·
parenthesis   —·——·—
underline   ··——·—

Morse code

Dictionaries present these "extra" kinds of information in one of two ways. Usually, some of the special information is given in sections at the front or the back of the dictionary. Lists of grammar rules usually will appear in a special section separate from the word entries.

A second way of presenting such information is to include it in the body of the dictionary, among the word entries. For example, names of famous people or geographical places may be mixed in among word entries in the body of one dictionary, or they may fall in separate sections at the back of another dictionary.

To find out where you can find various kinds of information in your own dictionary, you should preview it, just as you would preview a textbook. Look at the table of contents and the introductory material. Then leaf through the pages, from front to back. If your dictionary has cut-out alphabet guides, you may also find guides for biographical (people) and geographical (places) lists.

Activity 8–8 gives you a chance to explore your dictionary for different kinds of information. On a separate sheet of paper, number from one to ten. Use the dictionary entries provided to answer the questions that follow.

1. Who was James Buchanan?

2. What is the capital of Brazil?

3. Draw a picture of the configuration of a benzene ring.

4. What is the pattern of sound for an *I* in Morse Code?

5. What does the abbreviation *a.k.a.* stand for?

6. What does the abbreviation *ASAP* stand for?

7. What is the formula for benzoic acid?

8. What was Buffalo Bill's real name?

9. What does the dictionary say about Bunker Hill?

10. When was George Bush born?

Buchanan | Cartier

Bu·chan·an (byōō-kǎn'ən, bə-), James. 1791-1868. 15th U.S. President (1857-61).

Buck (bǔk), Pearl Sydenstricker. 1892-1973. Amer. author.

Bud·dha (bōō'də, bōōd'ə). 563?-483? B.C. Indian philosopher; founder of Buddhism. —Bud'dhist n. & adj.

Buf·fa·lo Bill (bǔf'ə-lō' bǐl'). William Frederick Cody.

Buf·fon (bü-fôn'). Comte Georges Louis Leclerc de. 1707-88. French naturalist.

Bu·kha·rin (bōō-KHä'rǐn), Nikolai Ivanovich. 1888-1938. Russian revolutionary.

Bur·ton (bûrt'n). 1. Robert. 1577-1640. English clergyman and author. 2. Sir Richard Francis. 1821-90. English Orientalist and adventurer.

Bush (bōōsh), George Herbert Walker. b. 1924. U.S. Vice President (since 1981).

But·ler (bǔt'lər), Samuel. 1835-1902. English novelist.

861

AK Alaska.
a.k.a. also known as.
AKC American Kennel Club.
AL 1. Alabama. 2. American League. 3. American Legion.

art. 1. article. 2. artillery.
arty. artillery.
As. Asia; Asian.
a/s airspeed.
ASAP also asap as soon as possible.

AK | bact.

Bolivia | Byzantine Empire

829

Bra·zil (brə-zǐl'). Country of E South America. Cap. Brasilia. Pop. 107,145,200. —Bra·zil'ian adj. & n.

Bra·zos (brǎz'əs, brä'zəs). River of E Tex., flowing c. 950 mi (1,528 km) to the Gulf of Mexico.

Braz·za·ville (brǎz'ə-vǐl'). Cap. of Congo, on the N bank of the Congo. Pop. 175,000.

Bre·men (brěm'ən). City of N West Germany, on the Weser R. Pop. 556,128.

Bren·ner Pass (brěn'ər). Alpine pass between S Austria and NE Italy.

Bre·scia (brě'shä). Industrial city of N central Italy. Pop. 212,265.

Brest (brěst). Also Brest Li·tovsk (lǐ-tôfsk', -tôvsk'). City of W European USSR. Pop. 186,000.

Bridge·port (brǐj'pôrt', -pōrt'). Industrial city of SW Conn. Pop. 142,546.

Bridge·town (brǐj'toun'). Cap. of Barbados, E West Indies. Pop. 8,789.

Brigh·ton (brīt'n). Seaside resort of SE England, on the English Channel. Pop. 152,700.

Bun·ker Hill (bǔng'kər). Hill in Charlestown, Mass., near site of 1st major Revolutionary War battle (1775).

Bur·gun·dy (bûr'gən-dē). Region and former duchy and province of SE France. —Burgun'di·an (bər-gǔn'dē-ən) adj. & n.

Bur·ling·ton (bûr'lǐng-tən). City of NW Vt., on Lake Champlain. Pop. 37,712.

Bur·ma (bûr'mə). Country of SE Asia on the E shore of the Bay of Bengal and the Andaman Sea. Cap. Rangoon. Pop. 31,512,000. —Bur·mese' (bər-mēz', -mēs') or Bur'man adj. & n.

Bur·na·by (bûr'nə-bē). City of SW B.C., Canada, near Vancouver. Pop. 131,599.

Bur·sa (bōōr-sä', bûr'sə). City of NW Turkey, near the Sea of Marmara. Pop. 466,178.

Bu·run·di (bōō-rōōn'dē). Country of E central Africa. Cap. Bujumbura. Pop. 3,864,000.

Byd·goszcz (bǐd'gôshch). Industrial city of N Poland. Pop. 343,800.

Byz·an·tine Empire (bǐz'ən-tēn', -tīn'). E part of the later Roman Empire.

---

bender | berth

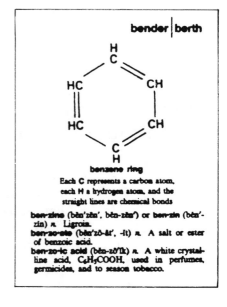

benzene ring

Each C represents a carbon atom, each H a hydrogen atom, and the straight lines are chemical bonds

ben·zine (běn'zēn', běn-zēn') or ben·zin (běn'-zǐn) n. Ligroin.

ben·zo·ate (běn'zō-āt', -ǐt) n. A salt or ester of benzoic acid.

ben·zo·ic acid (běn-zō'ǐk) n. A white crystalline acid, C_6H_5COOH, used in perfumes, germicides, and to season tobacco.

Activity 8–9
Homographs

The words in bold letters in the sentences below are homographs. On a separate sheet of paper, number from one to eleven. Beside each number write the letter of the dictionary entry that correctly identifies the homograph as it is used in the sentence. The first has been done as an example.

A. bark—the sound a dog makes

B. bark—the outer covering of a tree

C. bark—a sailing ship with three to five masts

    1. Early settlers in America arrived in a **bark**.   **Answer: C**

    2. The **bark** was stripped from the aspen by a deer.

A. buffer—an implement used to shine or polish

B. buffer—something that lessens or absorbs the shock of impact

    3. The wall acted as a **buffer** and protected her from the oncoming car.

A. bunting—a light cloth used for making flags

B. bunting—a bird with a short, cone-shaped bill

C. bunting—a hooded sleeping bag for infants

    4. The baby was wrapped in a **bunting**.

    5. Betsy Ross may have used **bunting** in her first sewing project.

A. case—a specified instance

B. case—a container or receptacle

    6. The detective solved the **case** after discovering one more clue.

A. pit—a relatively deep hole in the ground

B. pit—the single, hard-shelled seed of certain fruits

    7. Unfamiliar with the land, he fell into the **pit**.

A. prop—a support or stay

B. prop—a stage property

C. prop—a propeller

    8. She used the crutch as a **prop**.

    9. The director said the **prop** for Scene Two was inappropriate.

A. **pry**—to look closely; to snoop

B. **pry**—to raise, move, or force open with a lever

   10. He angrily accused his neighbor of trying to **pry**.

A. **rent**—periodic payment in return for the right to use the property of another

B. **rent**—an opening made by a rip

   11. The gale-force winds left a gaping **rent** in the curtain.

Activity 8–10
Unit Review

In Unit 8, you have practiced using dictionary entries to find information about words and about people and places, as well. You might have been surprised to learn just how much information your dictionary contains. Using what you now know and the dictionary entries provided, answer the following questions. On a separate sheet of paper, number from one to fifteen, and begin.

1. Define *main entry*.
2. Define *syllabication*.
3. Syllabicate the word *dependent*.
4. Define *variant spellings*.
5. Give the variant spelling of the word *dependent*.
6. Define *etymology*.
7. Give the etymology of the word *deplete*.
8. What is the etymological meaning of the word *deplete?*
9. Define *inflected form*.
10. Give the inflected form of the word *deplane*.
11. Define *guide words*.
12. List the guide words for this dictionary entry page.
13. Define *homograph*.
14. List three parts of speech.
15. List all the parts of speech for the word *dependent*.

Exploring the Library/Media Center

EXPLORE (ĕk-splōr') v. To investigate systematically

LIBRARY (lī'brĕr-ē) n. a repository for literary and artistic materials kept for reading or reference

MEDIA (mē'dē-ă) n. the agency by which something is conveyed or transferred

CENTER (sĕn'tər) n. a place of concentrated activity or influence

hat is it that you want to know? Maybe you have a term paper assignment and you need material on the life of Ernest Hemingway. Perhaps you are interested in collared lizards and don't know where to begin looking for information about them. To settle a bet you made with a friend, you may need to know how many home runs Dave Winfield hit in the 1983 World Series. No matter what kind of information you seek, the library/media center is the place to begin looking.

Library/media centers are designed with your needs as a student in mind. Why, then, is the card catalog a mystery? Why is searching a periodical index such an ordeal? And why is reading on microfilm a back issue of the newspaper so confusing? If the thought of having to go to your local library to do any of these makes you want to run for the door, relax and get comfortable, instead. This unit is designed to quickly and painlessly acquaint you with library services and materials.

Though libraries vary in arrangements, each has a collection that includes books, periodicals, microforms, and pamphlet materials. Some collections also include records, tapes, and videos, as well. The card catalog and other periodical indexes contain information to help you locate the various materials.

Your librarian can also help. Librarians and their assistants are there to make sure that the information you need is available to you. Of course, if you don't ask them questions, librarians can't know your needs. Don't be shy! There is no such thing as a dumb question.

A librarian can help you find information and also suggest sources you might not have considered.

Activity 9–1
Classification of Fiction

In most school and public libraries, books are classified and arranged on the shelves under the categories of fiction or nonfiction. Activity 9–1 deals with fiction books; Activity 9–2 discusses nonfiction books.

Writing that is based on imagination—that is not true—is called *fiction.* Fiction includes novels and short stories. In a library, fiction books are arranged alphabetically by the author's last name. For example, a book by James Michener will be found under the letter *M.* Collections of short stories written by several authors are arranged alphabetically by the collection editor's name.

Number a separate sheet of paper from one to five and arrange the following fiction books in the order they would appear on the library shelves.

1. *Siege of Silence* by A. J. Quinell

2. *The Land That Time Forgot* by E. R. Burroughs

3. *Follow the River* by J. A. Thom

4. *The Monkey Wrench Gang* by E. Abbey

5. *The Warrior's Path* by L. L'Amour

Activity 9–2
Classification of Nonfiction

A second major category of books on the shelves in library/media centers is the nonfiction category.

All books that are not novels or short stories—that are factual—are labeled *nonfiction*. Nonfiction materials are organized by two main classification systems: the Dewey decimal system, which uses numbers for identifying ten major subject categories, and the Library of Congress system, which uses letters for identifying twenty-one major categories. (See examples below.)

It is not important that you memorize either classification system. Just be aware that both systems are used, and that the LOC (Library of Congress) system is usually used in larger city and university libraries.

ABBREVIATED DEWEY DECIMAL CLASSIFICATION SCHEME

000–099	General Works
100–199	Philosophy and Psychology
200–299	Religion
300–399	Social Sciences
400–499	Language
500–599	Pure Sciences
600–699	Technology
700–799	The Arts
800–899	Literature
900–999	History

ABBREVIATED LIBRARY OF CONGRESS CLASSIFICATION SCHEME

A . . . . General Works
B . . . . Philosophy, Psychology, Religion
C . . . . History: Auxiliary Sciences (Archaeology, Numismatics, Genealogy, etc.)
D . . . . History: General and Old World
E . . . . History: American and U.S., general
F . . . . History: American and U.S., local
G . . . . Geography, Anthropology, Folklore, Dance, Sports
H . . . . Social Sciences: Sociology, Business, and Economics
J . . . . Political Science
K . . . . Law
L . . . . Education
M . . . . Music
N . . . . Fine Arts: Art and Architecture
P . . . . Literature
Q . . . . Science
R . . . . Medicine
S . . . . Agriculture
T . . . . Technology
U . . . . Military Science
V . . . . Naval Science
Z . . . . Bibliography and Library Science

Continuing on a separate sheet of paper, number from one to five again. List the identifying codes for the major categories in which books on the following topics would be found. Look at the classification schemes for the Dewey decimal system to help you decide.

1. Buddhism

2. Civil War (U.S.)

3. Mental disorders

4. Conversational Dutch

5. Modern music

Activity 9–3
Reading Call Numbers

In all libraries, nonfiction books are arranged on the shelves, or stacks, by their call numbers. Each book has its own call number made up of its classification code (either Dewey decimal or Library of Congress), as well as its own letter-number combinations, which indicates the book's author.

Dewey decimal call numbers should be read one line at a time. *Example:*

Complete call number 527.6 . . . . . . Line One (classification)
J53 . . . . Line Two (author)

The books are first arranged numerically, according to the numbers in Line One.
Example:

Line One   515 | 519.3 | 520 | 525 | 526.4 | 527.6

The arrangement of Line Two is first alphabetical and then numerical, with the number in Line Two being read as a decimal number. Read J.3 followed by J.34 followed by J.4. **Example:**

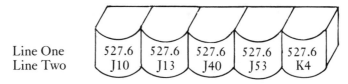

Line One
Line Two

The following numbers are call numbers of books classified under the Dewey decimal system. Arrange them in the correct order by call number, as if they were actual books. Then, using the ten main divisions of the Dewey decimal system, name the category to which each book would belong.

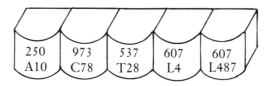

Activity 9–4
Determining Classification Groups Using Titles

The following titles clearly reveal their subject matter. List the authors and titles on the separate sheet of paper you are using. Opposite each, write the Dewey decimal classification group to which it belongs.

1. John Carroll, *The Study of Language*

2. J. Newton Friend, *Man and the Chemical Element*

3. Harry Emerson Fosdick, *The Man from Nazareth*

4. John Gunther, *Inside Latin America*

5. Ivor Brown, *Shakespeare in His Time*

Activity 9–5
Determining Classification Groups Using Dewey Numbers

The titles in the following list do not clearly indicate the subjects of the books. Determine the subject matter of each book by comparing the Dewey classification number after each title with the Dewey classification list. Number from one to five on a separate sheet of paper and write the letter of the correct answer beside the appropriate number.

1. *I Can Jump Puddles* (616)

   A. a novel

   B. a biography

   C. a book telling how a polio victim overcame hardships

2. *The Wild Duck* (808.8)

    A. a scientific book for biology class

    B. a book on hunting wild game

    C. a play

3. *The Crack in the Picture Window* (711)

    A. the history of glass

    B. an inquiry into the architecture of American housing developments

    C. a history of government foreclosures of mortgages

4. *Journey Into Light* (617.7)

    A. a biography

    B. the story of medical help for the blind

    C. a travel book

5. *Horsefeathers* (422)

    A. a book dealing with word origins

    B. a book of party games

    C. a book of veterinary medicine

Activity 9–6
Understanding the Card Catalog

The easiest way to find the books you want in the library is by using the card catalog. The card catalog contains alphabetically arranged cards listing the call numbers of each book in the library's collection. There are usually three cards for each book: an author card, a title card, and a subject card. You may also find a cross-reference card, referring you to another related topic listed in the card catalog.

    The catalog cards also list information such as the book's publisher, the publication date, the number of pages, and whether the book includes illustrations.

Subject Card

OWLS
598.97 Austing, G. Ronald
The World of the Great Horned Owl: Text and photographs by G. Ronald Austing and John B. Holt, Jr. New York: Lippincott, c 1968.
158 pp. illus. (Living World Books)

Title Card

The World of the Great Horned Owl.
598.97   Text and photographs by G. Ronald Austing and
John B. Holt, Jr. New York: Lippincott, c. 1968.
158 pp. illus. (Living World Books)

Author Card

Austing, G. Ronald
598.97   The World of the Great Horned Owl: Text and
photographs by G. Ronald Austing and John B.
Holt, Jr. New York: Lippincott, c 1968.
158 pp. illus. (Living World Books)
1. Owls 2. Birds, predator

Cross-reference Card

OWLS
see also
Birds, predator

Refer to the previous examples of cards from the card catalog for the book on owls. Number a separate sheet of paper from one to ten and try to answer the following questions:

1. What three ways are books usually listed in the card catalog?

2. What is the title of the book?

3. Who wrote the book?

4. Who is the publisher?

5. When was the book published?

6. What kind of a book does the Dewey decimal call number indicate it is?

7. Who was the photographer for this book?

8. How many pages does this book have?

9. What series is this book a part of?

10. What is another cross-reference other than the one given that might apply to owls?

The reference section contains a wealth of information.

Activity 9–7
Using the Card Catalog

Number a separate sheet of paper from one to five. Using the card catalog in your library/media center, find the author, title, and call number for each of the following:

1. A book written *by* Samuel Clemens (Mark Twain)

2. A book written *about* Samuel Clemens

3. A nonfiction book written about Africa

4. A collection of American poetry

5. A book about space travel

Activity 9–8
Using Reference Materials

Reference books are valuable information sources usually kept together in the reference section of the library. They must be used in the library; they cannot be checked out.

Before attempting to use any reference book for the first time, skim its introductory pages to learn how to use it and how to decode the symbols and other abbreviations used in that particular volume. Reference books include:

Dictionaries
In addition to the familiar collection of words and definitions, there are dictionaries on languages, medicine, math, and music, to name only a few.

Encyclopedias
Encyclopedias are one of the best places to begin looking for research materials. Here you will find articles on a variety of subjects written by experts. Topics are arranged alphabetically; the letters on the spine of each volume indicate the portion of the alphabet that volume covers.

Almanacs and Yearbooks
These volumes, published annually, summarize the previous year's events. They contain factual and statistical information on current developments in such areas as government, sports, economics, careers, and so on.

Biographical Reference Books
These books offer brief biographical sketches of notable people in all fields, worldwide. Some list living, currently prominent persons, while others refer to specific groups, such as actors or presidents.

Literary Reference Books and Books About Authors
Anything you need to know concerning literature can be found under this category. Find who wrote it or said it or where it came from by consulting such volumes as *Twentieth Century Authors, Bartlett's Familiar Quotations, Granger's Index to Poetry,* and *The Oxford Companion to American Literature.*

Periodicals
When doing research, you'll often find newspapers, magazines, and digests quite useful. They may be used to supplement information you find in books, or, for certain topics, they may be the only information source available. Some libraries keep back issues of periodicals on microforms (microfilm and microfiche) for convenient storage. Current events digests such as *Facts on File, A Matter of Fact,* and *Social Issues Resources Series, Inc. (SIRS)* are available in some libraries.

Maps and Atlases
Most libraries have a selection of atlases containing a variety of interesting data and maps. Where do Kudus roam when they are not in a zoo? Check the *Atlas of World Wildlife.* What is the highest mountain peak on each continent? Look in the *Rand McNally World Atlas.*

Vertical File

Usually found in filing cabinets accessible to library users, the vertical file contains the "et cetera" category in most libraries. This is the place you will find small pamphlets, booklets, catalogs, and clippings on a variety of topics. Depending on the rules at your library, information from the vertical file may sometimes be checked out.

Because you'll use them often, it's important to know where in your library the reference area is and what particular reference volumes are available there. To help you find out, take a trip to the reference area of your library and, on a separate sheet of paper, write the answers to the following questions. Be sure to note both the titles and page numbers of the reference books you use, as well as the answer to each question.

1. What is the height of the Statue of Liberty?

2. When is Richard Burton's birthday?

3. What is the difference in elevation between the highest and lowest points in the United States?

4. What is the language spoken in Jordan?

5. From what language do we get the word *recipe*?

6. Who is the author and what is the title of a poem in which these lines appear:
    "And what is so rare as a day in June?
    Then, if ever, came perfect days . . . ."

7. List the title of a catalog found in the vertical file.

8. What type of sporting events are featured in the latest issue of a newspaper kept in your library?

9. List the titles of two magazines that include information on health and nutrition.

10. What was the year women were first allowed to vote for the president of the United States? Who was elected that year?

Activity 9–9
Periodical Indexes

When you need to locate articles on a specific subject, you can sit down and browse through piles of magazines and stacks of newspapers. Or, you can save time and consult a periodical index. Periodical indexes enable you to find material on a given topic or by a specific author quickly.

At your local library, you may have access to the *Readers' Guide to Periodical Literature* in bound volumes, or you may be able to use an Infotrac system consisting of a computer and a compact disk. Either way, if you could compare the two you would find that they use basically the same form of entry.

An entry in the *Readers' Guide* or on Infotrac is called a *citation*. Once you understand the format, you can read the citations easily. A citation looks something like this:

Readers' Guide Citation

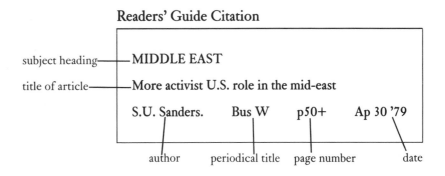

subject heading——— MIDDLE EAST

title of article——— More activist U.S. role in the mid-east

S.U. Sanders.   Bus W   p50+   Ap 30 '79

author   periodical title   page number   date

Infotrac Citation

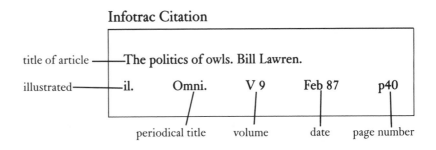

title of article ——— The politics of owls. Bill Lawren.

illustrated——— il.   Omni.   V 9   Feb 87   p40

periodical title   volume   date   page number

Periodical indexes help you find materials on a specific topic quickly.

Notice that each citation includes abbreviations. Some, like the examples given, are very easy to decipher. Others, however, are more difficult, so always check the list of abbreviations given at the beginning of the index for a complete translation.

As you do research, get in the habit of writing down the entire citation, along with the title of the index in which you found it. This will simplify your task when you have to list the sources of your information.

As you can imagine, storage is becoming an ever-increasing problem in this age of mass communication. Many libraries use microforms to solve storage problems. The term *microform* describes information that has been photographed and reduced in size. Libraries often store newspapers and magazines on microfiche or microfilm—two types of microforms frequently used. Special machines called *readers,* some equipped with printers, are required in order for you to use the microforms. Ask your librarian to help you learn to use the reader machine.

The names of the publications found in the microform collection are sometimes listed in the card catalog. Other libraries list microforms in a special catalog. No matter where you find the cards in your library, they will look something like this:

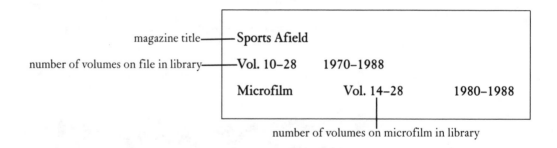

Now that you are more familiar with periodical indexes, number a separate sheet of paper from one to ten and list two complete citations for each of the following topics. Use the *Readers' Guide to Periodical Literature* or Infotrac to find the magazine articles.

A. TV advertising   D. baseball

B. environmental control   E. elections

C. photography

Activity 9–10
Using the *Readers' Guide to Periodical Literature*

Using the sample pages from the *Readers' Guide*, list the names of the magazines that include articles on the following topics. If there is more than one article for the topic, list only the first magazine.

A. sports cars—design   D. stars—age

B. sports medicine   E. stars—new

C. stage fright   F. List the complete citation for an article on Bruce Springsteen that includes illustrations.

Activity 9–11
Mini Research Project

Now you can practice your newly acquired library skills. We have carefully divided the project into manageable steps. You'll need to allow several hours to complete this project. You must have access to a library as you work. Follow these steps:

A. **Choose a topic that interests you.** You may know very little or a lot about this topic, but you should definitely choose a topic you want to know more about. Be specific rather than broad in your choice of topic.

B. **Do the research.**

1. Look up the topic in either the *Readers' Guide* or on Infotrac.

2. List three or four complete citations for your topic. If you limit yourself to one article, that periodical might not be available, and you will have to begin again.

3. Check the periodicals listed in your citations against the "Magazine Holdings Directory" (a list of magazines in your library) to be sure that your library has that particular periodical available. (No library has funds or room for all the periodicals published.)

4. For each citation, you will be asked to fill out a periodical request slip that looks something like this:

PERIODICAL REQUEST SLIP

Name of Magazine _____

Date of Issue: Month _____ Day ____ Year ____

Volume _____ Page _____

Your name _____

SPORTS CARS—Design—*cont.*
New Ferrari seen—despite denials. il *Motor Trend* 40:24 My '88
History
Carrera RS 2.7 [Porsche] J. Rusz. il *Road & Track* 39:55 My '88
Learning the hard way [TVR] P. Bingham. il *Motor Trend* 40:118-19 My '88
Testing
Chevrolet Corvette [cover story] C. Csere. il *Car and Driver* 33:44-8+ My '88
Porsche 911 Club Sport [cover story] il *Road & Track* 39:50-4 My '88
Porsche 944 Turbo S. J. Karr. il *Motor Trend* 40:72-3+ My '88
The Schwarzenegger of muscle cars [Corvette] W. J. Hampton. il *Business Week* p161 My 9 '88
SPORTS CARS, RACING *See* Automobiles, Racing
SPORTS CLUBS
See also
Achilles Track Club
Atoms Track Club
How to be a social smash: smart sets [tennis clubs; special section] il *Harper's Bazaar* 121:142-5+ My '88
SPORTS FANS
See also
Baseball fans
Boxing fans
SPORTS JOURNALISM
Hoops but no scoops [press coverage restricted at U.S. Olympic basketball trials] A. Wolff. il *Sports Illustrated* 68:34-6 My 30 '88
Seduced and abandoned [poor press coverage of stock car racing] A. Girdler. il *Road & Track* 39:28 My '88
SPORTS MANAGEMENT *See* Sports—Organization and administration
SPORTS MEDICINE
See also
Running—Accidents and injuries
Tennis—Accidents and injuries
Pain, pain, go away. D. Groves. il *Women's Sports & Fitness* 10:32-4 Ap '88
SPORTS OFFICIATING
See also
Baseball, Professional—Umpiring
Hockey, Professional—Refereeing
Tennis—Tournaments—Officiating
SPORTS RECORDS
See also
Boat speed records
Fishing records
SPORTS SHOES *See* Footwear
SPORTS WRITING *See* Sports journalism
SPORTSCASTERS *See* Cable television—Sports; Radio broadcasting—Sports; Television broadcasting—Sports
SPORTSMEN *See* Athletes
SPORTSMIND (FIRM)
Breaking through. J. Harris. il *Esquire* 109:154-7 My '88
SPORTSWOMEN *See* Women athletes
SPORTSWRITING *See* Sports journalism
SPRADLING, RICHARD
(jt. auth) *See* Buford, Constance W., and Spradling, Richard
SPRAYING AND DUSTING
See also
Pesticides
SPREADS (FOOD)
Camembert spread with walnut flat bread. il *Better Homes and Gardens* 66:118+ Ap '88
Haroseth: versatile sweet fruit spread [Passover tradition] il *Better Homes and Gardens* 66:143+ Ap '88
SPREADSHEETS (COMPUTER PROGRAMS)
Testing
Moving to a new dimension [Boeing Calc] M. Bryan. il *Personal Computing* 12:220 Ap '88
SPRING
See also
May
SPRING CLEANING *See* House cleaning
SPRING DINNERS *See* Dinners and dining
SPRINGER, NANCY
Sparrow's fall [story] il *U.S. Catholic* 53:32-7 Ap '88
SPRINGFIELD (MASS.)
Economic conditions
The Springfield 'miracle'. J. Nocera. il *Newsweek* 111:45-6+ Je 6 '88

SPRINGSTEEN, BRUCE
Tangled up in Bob [address, January 20, 1988] *Harper's* 276:28-9+ Ap '88
about
Bruce Springsteen's Tunnel vision [cover story] S. Pond. il pors *Rolling Stone* p38-42 My 5 '88
SPRINT (WORD PROCESSOR PROGRAM) *See* Word processors and processing—Programming
SPRINTING *See* Track and field athletics
SPROCKETT, DOC
Battery power. *Flower and Garden* 32:91-2 Ap/My '88
SQL (STRUCTURED QUERY LANGUAGE) *See* Structured Query Language (Computer language)
SQUAB COOKING *See* Cooking—Poultry
SSC *See* Superconducting Super Collider
SSMC INC.
Can Paul Bilzerian fatten Singer for the kill? R. Mitchell. il por *Business Week* p43-4 My 16 '88
ST. ELSEWHERE [television program] *See* Television program reviews—Single works
ST. LOUIS (MO.) *See* Saint Louis (Mo.)
ST. PAUL'S CATHEDRAL CHOIR
Musical events:
Concert in St. Bartholomew's Church in New York. A. Porter. *The New Yorker* 64:98-9 My 16 '88
STABILITY OF AUTOMOBILES *See* Automobiles—Stability and stabilizers
STABLES, CONVERTED *See* Houses, Remodeled
STACHYS BYZANTINA *See* Lambs ears (Plant)
STADD, COURTNEY
about
Commercializing space: a conversation with Courtney Stadd. J. Muncy. por *Space World* Y-5-293:23-6 My '88
STADIUM ORGANISTS *See* Organists
STAGE *See* Theater
STAGE FRIGHT
Curing stage fright [musicians; research by Duncan Clark] *USA Today (Periodical)* 116:11 Ap '88
STAGE WEST THEATRE RESTAURANTS
An appetite for hits. P. Young. il *Maclean's* 101:50 My 23 '88
STAIRCASES *See* Stairways
STAIRWAYS
See also
Hand railings
Upgrade of unsafe stairway. D. Johnson. il *The Family Handyman* 38:82-3 My/Je '88
STALIN, JOSEPH, 1879-1953
about
A conversation with Stalin. V. V. Karpov. il *New Perspectives Quarterly* 5:51-3 Spr '88
STALKER, JOHN
Grave lies [excerpt from The Stalker affair] il *Life* 11:154+ My '88
STALLONE, JACQUELINE
about
Yo, mama! The wrestling Stallone, Sly's mother, Jackie, returns to the ring with a stable of Rambettes. S. K. Reed. il pors *People Weekly* 29:96-8 My 23 '88
STALLS, AIRPLANE *See* Airplanes, Business—Stalling
STAMINA *See* Endurance
STAMPS, POSTAGE *See* Postage stamps
STANDARD OIL CO. (OHIO)
See also
Standard Oil Company
STANDARD OIL COMPANY
Hearst's little time bomb [incriminating letters by J. D. Archbold of Standard Oil Company to various state and federal officials acquired by W. R. Hearst] P. Baida. il por *American Heritage* 39:18-19+ Ap '88
STANDS (MACHINE) *See* Machinery—Stands, tables, etc.
STANFORD UNIVERSITY
Excellence under the palm trees. T. A. Sancton. il *Time* 131:74-6 My 16 '88
Why the West? [defense of Western civilization] W. J. Bennett. il *National Review* 40:37-9 My 27 '88
STANFORD UNIVERSITY PRESS
Stanford to publish massive collection of London's letters. W. Goldstein. *Publishers Weekly* 233:36-7 Ap 29 '88
STAPHYLOCOCCAL DISEASES
See also
Toxic shock syndrome
STAR CHARTS *See* Astronomy—Charts, diagrams, etc.
STAR MAPS *See* Astronomy—Charts, diagrams, etc.
STAR WARS DEFENSE PROGRAM *See* Strategic Defense Initiative
STARCH
See also
Cornstarch

STARCK, PHILIPPE, 1950?-
about
Starck reality. L. Campbell. il *House & Garden* 160:38-40
Mr '88
STARGARDT'S DISEASE
Starring in track, tennis and soccer, Laurinda Mulhaupt
won't let blindness put her on the sidelines. K. Gross.
il pors *People Weekly* 29:119-21 My 23 '88
STARK, ELIZABETH
Beyond rivalry. il *Psychology Today* 22:61-3 Ap '88
STARR, DOUGLAS
Preserving pieces of the puzzle. il *National Wildlife* 26:4-13
Ap/My '88
STARR, JEROLD M., 1941-
A curriculum for teaching about the Vietnam War. *The
Education Digest* 53:28-31 Ap '88
STARS
See also
Astrology
Astronomy
Black holes (Astronomy)
Constellations
Galaxies
Age
How old is the Milky Way? *Sky and Telescope* 75:463-4
My '88
Charts, diagrams, etc.
See Astronomy—Charts, diagrams, etc.
Evolution
See also
Pulsars
Cosmic cloud without a heart [W49A star-forming region;
research by William John Welch and others] il *Discover*
9:10+ Ap '88
Journeys on the H-R diagram. J. B. Kaler. il *Sky and
Telescope* 75:482-5 My '88
Magnetic properties
Giant starspots on Lambda Andromedae [research by
James C. Kemp] *Sky and Telescope* 75:465-6 My '88
STARS, DOUBLE
New explanation for an old nova [Nova Cygni 1975;
research by Peter Stockman and others] D. E. Thomsen.
Science News 133:229 Ap 9 '88
STARS, NEW
New explanation for an old nova [Nova Cygni 1975;
research by Peter Stockman and others] D. E. Thomsen.
Science News 133:229 Ap 9 '88
STARS, VARIABLE
See also
Supernovas
Giant starspots on Lambda Andromedae [research by
James C. Kemp] *Sky and Telescope* 75:465-6 My '88
STARS AND BARS [film] *See* Motion picture
reviews—Single works
STARSHIP AIRPLANES *See* Airplanes, Business
START TALKS *See* Strategic Arms Reduction Talks
STARVATION
See also
Famines
STATE AND ART *See* Art and state
STATE AND CHURCH *See* Church and state
STATE AND EDUCATION *See* Education and state
STATE AND ENVIRONMENT *See* Environmental policy
STATE AND INDUSTRY *See* Industry and state
STATE AND LIBRARIES *See* Libraries and state
STATE AND LITERATURE *See* Literature and state
STATE AND MEDICINE *See* Medical policy
STATE AND SCIENCE *See* Science and state
STATE COURTS *See* Courts
STATE DEPT. (U.S.) *See* United States. Dept. of State
STATE EMPLOYEES
See also
AFSCME
STATE FINANCE
See also
Finance—Massachusetts
Big states, big gaps. T. Smart and H. Gleckman. il *Business
Week* p30-1 Je 6 '88
STATE SALES TAX *See* Sales tax
STATES, IDEAL *See* Utopias
STATES (U.S.)
States and Capitals [educational video games] E. Larsen
and M. D. Perry, Jr. il *Compute!* 10:80-2 Ap '88
STATHOPLOS, DEMMIE
One heavenly Star. il *Sports Illustrated* 68:32-3 My 30
'88
STATIC ELECTRICITY
How to map electrically charged patches with parsley,
sage, rosemary and thyme. J. Walker. il *Scientific
American* 258:114-17 Ap '88

STATMAN, MARK
(jt. auth) *See* Doyle, Kate, and Statman, Mark
STAUB, AUGUST W.
The mandate of the arts educator for cultural leadership:
somewhere between catering and contempt. *Design for
Arts in Education* 89:48-50 Mr/Ap '88
STAVOLE, NADINE
about
I showed my body who's boss! il pors *Mademoiselle*
94:60 Ap '88
STEAK COOKING *See* Cooking—Meat
STEALING
See also
Art thefts
Cattle—Theft
Credit card crimes
Embezzlement
STEALTH AIRPLANES *See* Airplanes, Military
STEAMSHIPS AND STEAMBOATS
See also
Ocean liners
STEARIC ACID
The good news about 'good fat' [stearic acid found to
lower cholesterol] il *U.S. News & World Report*
104:12-13 My 23 '88
Meaty matters [stearic acid found to lower cholesterol]
il *Time* 131:79 My 23 '88
STEEL, RONALD
Why a Democrat can't end the cold war. il *New
Perspectives Quarterly* 5:39-43 Spr '88
STEEL INDUSTRY
See also
McLouth Steel Products Corporation
United Steelworkers of America
STEEL SHOT *See* Shot
STEEL WORKERS
See also
United Steelworkers of America
STEELSMITH, RICK
about
Rick's got some tricks. J. Garrity. il pors *Sports Illustrated*
68:71-2+ My 9 '88
STEGER, WILL
North to the Pole [condensation]; ed. by Paul Schurke.
il *Reader's Digest* 132:229-34+ My '88
STEGMAIER, MARK E.
Gary Bowling. il *American Artist* 52:56-61+ My '88
STEHLIN, DORI
The silent epidemic of hip fractures. il *FDA Consumer*
22:18-23 My '88
STEIN, FRANCES PATIKY
about
Jet-set extras. il por *Harper's Bazaar* 121:40 My '88
STEIN, HARRY
Mates for life [excerpt from One of the guys] il *Glamour*
85:106+ Ap '88
STEIN, MARVIN, AND ABRAMS, MAXINE
How to stop making yourself sick. il *Good Housekeeping*
206:72+ Ap '88
STEIN, SUSAN R., 1949-
Thomas Jefferson's traveling desks. bibl f il *Antiques*
133:1156-9 My '88
STEINBACH, HAIM
about
Haim Steinbach: shelf life. H. Cotter. bibl f il *Art in
America* 76:156-63+ My '88
STEINBERG, LILLI
about
Refund sleuth Lilli Steinberg wrings money from phone
bills. il por *People Weekly* 29:95 My 23 '88
STEINGARTEN, JEFFREY
Fish without fire. il *House & Garden* 160:176-7+ Mr
'88
Takeout heaven? il *House & Garden* 160:156-7+ Ap '88
STEMPEL, ROBERT C.
about
GM faces reality [cover story] J. B. Treece. il pors *Business
Week* p114-18+ My 9 '88
STENSIÖ, ERIK ANDERSSON
about
A tale of three pictures. S. J. Gould. il *Natural History*
97:14+ My '88
STEPAN, ALFRED
The last days of Pinochet? il por *The New York Review
of Books* 35:32-5 Je 2 '88
STEPS *See* Stairways
STEREO LOUDSPEAKERS *See* Loudspeakers
STEREO SOUND SYSTEMS *See* Audio systems
STEREOCHEMISTRY
See also
Conformational analysis

If the periodicals are not kept in open stacks, your librarian will get them for you.

5. *Save* the periodical request slips when you have the magazines or newspapers. You will need the slips to list your sources.

6. Read the articles carefully, taking notes on their contents.

C. Write the summary.

1. Write your name in the upper right-hand corner of a separate sheet of paper. Below that, list the name of this class and the date.

2. On the first line, in the center, write the title of your summary.

3. Using your notes, summarize what you have read. Make it interesting to your reader. Use your own words—not the author's.

4. On a separate sheet of paper entitled "Bibliography," list the complete citations for all of the articles you read to make your summary. Arrange the citations alphabetically according to magazine title.

5. Your instructor will want to see the periodical request slips you filled out, in addition to your summary and bibliography.

Activity 9–12 Unit Review

Number a separate sheet of paper from one to thirty. After reading the question and referring to the typed entry, select the correct multiple-choice answer or the appropriate answer to fill in the blank. Write your answer beside the corresponding number on your paper.

973.9

Lo

      Lord, Walter

        The good years; from 1900 to the first World War.

      Harper, 1960.

        369 p., illus., 32 plates, maps.

      1. U.S. - Civilization 2. U.S. History - 1898 3. Child

      Labor - U.S.

---

1. The card shown would be found in the card catalog filed under:

    A. Lo.   C. Wa.

    B. 973.9.   D. The.

2. The card shown is called a(n):

    A. title card.   C. subject card.

    B. author card.   D. all of the above

3. The author of the book is:

    A. Lord Walter.   C. Harper.

    B. Walter Lord.   D. none of the above

4. The title of the book is:

    A. Lord Walter.

    B. The good years; from 1900 to the first World War.

    C. The good years.

    D. none of the above

5. The subject of this book is:

    A. U.S.—Civilization.   C. Child Labor—U.S.

    B. U.S. History—1898.   D. all of the above

6. The call number of this book is:

    A. 973.9.   C. Lord.

    B. 973.9   D. none of the above
       Lo

7. The above book is:

    A. nonfiction.   C. reference.

    B. fiction.   D. none of the above

8. The book was published by _____.

9. It was published in _____.

10. The abbreviation *illus.* means _____.

790
Se

    DANCING
    Seaton, Don Cash
      Physical Education Handbook, 4th ed., Englewood
    Cliffs, N.J., Prentice-Hall, 1965. 3. Child Labor - U.S.
    365 p., illus.

11. The card shown is a(n):

    A. title card.   C. subject card.

    B. author card.   D. all of the above

12. If you were looking in the card catalog for the card shown, you would look in:

    A. the *Da* drawer.   C. the *Ph* drawer.

    B. the *Se* drawer.   D. all of the above

13. The author of this book is:

    A. Seaton Don Cash.   C. Seaton Cash Don.

    B. Don Cash Seaton.   D. Cash Don Seaton.

14. The title of the book is:
    A. Dancing.   C. Seaton, Don Cash.

    B. Physical Education   D. none of the above
       Handbook.

15. The call number of this book is:

    A. 790.   C. Seaton.

    B. 790   D. none of the above
       Se

16. The publisher is _____.

17. It was published in what year? _____.

18. *4th ed.* means _____.

SPACE Flight

        Manned flights

Charts may guide return from moon. H. Taylor.

Time   89:51   Je 25 '86

19. The title of the magazine article is:

    A. SPACE Flight.

    B. Manned flights.

    C. Charts may guide return from moon.

    D. none of the above

20. The subject of the article is:

    A. Manned flights.

    B. SPACE Flight.

    C. both of the above

    D. Charts may guide return from moon.

21. The author of the article is _____.

22. The name of the magazine is _____.

23. The volume number of the magazine is _____.

24. The page(s) the article is found on is (are) _____.

25. The date the magazine was published is _____.

> New way of living; excerpt from a new kind of
> country. il McCalls   105:193–200   My 19 '87

26. The title of the article is _____.

27. The article is taken from what larger work? _____

28. The article appears in what magazine? _____

29. Which volume? _____

30. What is the date of the magazine? _____

UNIT TEN

Reading for Enjoyment

READ (rēd), v. to comprehend the meaning of something written or printed

ENJOYMENT (in-joi'mənt), n. pleasure, satisfaction

ow long has it been since you read something for relaxation or fun? For many people, reading for pleasure is a rare treat—a chance to catch up on sports news, to learn how to do a weekend project, to get caught up in a mystery or science-fiction fantasy.

As you read and complete the activities in this unit, you will have opportunities to read your local newspaper, browse through a magazine, or get lost in a good book. The most important goal is to rekindle your enthusiasm for reading for pleasure.

Begin your reading for pleasure by sitting down with a copy of your local newspaper. Some of you will read metropolitan papers; others will read papers from small towns. As you read, notice the unique style of your local newspaper. Compare its format to that of one of your classmate's newspapers. Notice how the writing style varies from reporter to reporter. You'll find that newspapers contain a wealth of information beyond "Dear Abby," the comics, and the sports section. Avid reader or not, you will learn from and enjoy reading your local newspaper.

Activity 10–1
Newspaper Survey

This activity will help you to evaluate your reading habits regarding the daily newspaper. Using a separate sheet of paper, write your responses to the Newspaper Survey that follows. Your instructor may ask you to share your responses so you can compare your reading habits with those of your classmates.

Newspaper Survey

1. What newspaper(s) do you read?

2. How frequently do you read a newspaper?

3. What time of the day do you read the newspaper?

4. Indicate which newspaper sections you read and how often you read them by writing the name of the section and *always, usually, sometimes,* or *never* after each section you list.

front page	features
sports	classified ads
editorials	general ads
business	weather
comics	obituaries

5. If you didn't have the opportunity, would you miss reading the newspaper? If so, why?

Activity 10–2
Newspaper Jargon

There are some common terms used frequently by people discussing the newspaper. Knowing these terms will help you understand and actively participate in this part of the unit.

On a separate sheet of paper, write the terms that follow and their definitions. Then locate an example of each term in the newspaper of your choice. The terms listed below will appear again in the Unit Review, so be sure your notes on them are complete and accurate.

1. Banner Headline: a headline that stretches across the newspaper page from one side to the other.

2. Headline: large type above an article indicating the content of the article.

3. Byline: a line at the beginning of an article listing the author's name.

4. Dateline: a line indicating where the event described in the article took place.

5. News Agency: an organization that sends news stories by wire. Two of the most well-known news agencies are the Associated Press and the United Press International.

6. A.P.: the abbreviation for *Associated Press.*

7. U.P.I.: the abbreviation for *United Press International.*

8. Lead: an article's first paragraph, in which the questions *who, what, when, where,* and *why* are answered (the five Ws).

9. Caption: the words beside or below a photograph or illustration that give information about the picture.

10. Jump: words informing a reader that an article continues on another page.

Activity 10–3
Sections of the Newspaper

Take a minute and try to name all the sections you would find in an average newspaper. If you are the type of reader who skips from the front page to the sports section to the comics, you might have trouble with your list. This activity will help you discover *all* of the sections in your newspaper.

First, from the following list read the name of the newspaper section and its description. Add this information to your notes. Then, using a newspaper and its index, find that particular section. In your notes, write down the location in your newspaper of each of the sections given.

Sections of the Newspaper

Front Page: the page a reader sees first. Its format, appeal, and contents often influence a reader's decision about whether to buy the paper. Thus, the front page helps to sell the paper; it also carries the most important stories of the day.

Editorial Section: Presents opinions through editorials by staff writers; editorial cartoons; letters to the editor (written by readers); and syndicated columns.

Feature Section: Entertains and appeals to readers' interests through comics; information on and reviews of movies, plays, concerts, and celebrities; homemaking hints; fashion news; and so on.

Sports Section: Covers a wide variety of sports events and includes analyses of player and team performances; coaching strategies; scheduled games; statistics; predicted winners; and so on.

Business Section: Consists of articles that discuss and analyze economic activity; personnel; business strategies; and companies of note. It also includes stock quotations and interest rates.

Advertising Section: Pays those who produce the newspaper; allows businesses to communicate with consumers; informs readers of products and services available in the marketplace.

Weather Section: Includes local or regional forecasts; describes road conditions; lists national temperatures and extended forecasts.

Obituary Section: Contains notices of the deaths of prominent persons, usually members of the community, but sometimes national or international figures. It usually includes brief accounts of the persons' lives and may include lists of surviving family members and funeral information.

Activity 10–4
Analyzing the Newspaper

Too often people limit their newspaper reading to only a couple of sections. For example, when you read a newspaper, you may consistently read only the front page, the comics, and the list of automobiles for sale. But what valuable information are you missing by doing this? Activity 10–4 will show you.

Using a newspaper and its index, locate the sections of the newspaper discussed in the previous activity (Activity 10–3) in order to discover what type of information is contained in each section. Then, on a separate sheet of paper, answer the following questions:

Front Page

1. What is the title of the most important story on the newspaper's front page?

2. Does the front page have one or more pictures? Does it include an index?

3. How many articles appear on the front page?

Editorial Section

1. Does the editorial section contain letters to the editor? editorial cartoons? syndicated columns?

2. List the topic of one of the editorials written by a staff writer.

Feature Section

1. Does the feature section include a TV schedule? a movie schedule? a review of a movie? comics? hints for homemakers? fashion news? "Dear Abby" or "Ann Landers" columns?

Sports Section

1. Does the sports section include a sports cartoon? team standing? reports of past games? a story about an important person in sports? a column by a sports writer?

2. On what pages do you find sports information?

Business Section

1. Does the business section list stock quotations from the New York Stock Exchange? the American Stock Exchange? over-the-counter stocks?

2. Does the section contain articles about important people in business? specific companies? List the names of the companies featured.

3. Does the section contain syndicated columns? a report on grain prices? money market rates?

Advertising

1. On what pages do you find the classified ads?

Weather

1. On what pages do you find the weather discussed?

2. Does the weather section contain forecasts? road conditions? national temperatures?

Obituaries

1. On what pages do you find the obituaries?

2. Do any of the obituaries include pictures?

3. How many obituaries are listed in today's section?

Newspaper sections are devoted to different topics and interests.

Activity 10–5
Exploring the Front Page

Remember that a newspaper's front page is very important, especially on the newsstand. It must sell the paper. What do you know about the front page of today's newspaper? Use it to help you answer the questions that follow. Write your responses on a separate sheet of paper.

1. What is the headline of today's top news story?

2. How many columns does the front page of your newspaper have?

3. Does your newspaper print weather news on the front page?

4. Does your newspaper print an index on the front page?

5. How many front-page news stories contain a jump?

6. How many front-page stories have been circulated by news agencies? How many are from the A.P.? How many are from the U.P.I.?

7. How many photographs appear on the front page?

8. How many headlines on the front page of today's newspaper take up more than one column?

9. Does the front page contain a banner headline?

10. How many front-page stories contain bylines?

11. How much does your newspaper cost?

Activity 10–6
Exploring the Editorial Pages

You probably take time to read your newspaper's front page, but its editorial pages may be new to you. They present opinions of the newspaper's editorial staff, opinions of syndicated columnists from across the country, and opinions of the general public. By reading the editorial pages, you encounter new viewpoints. Whether you agree or disagree with what is being expressed, the editorials will make you think more about your position on the issue.

Using a separate sheet of paper and today's newspaper, turn to the editorial section and answer the following questions:

1. Find the editorials written by the newspaper's **editorial staff.** List headlines from two of them.

2. Choose one of the two editorials, explain the staff writer's viewpoint, and then discuss your viewpoint.

3. Find the **letters to the editor** and list the topics of two of the letters.

4. Choose one of the letters to the editor, explain how the author felt about the topic, and then discuss your feelings.

5. Study one of the **editorial cartoons** and then explain its theme.

6. Find two **syndicated columns.** List the headline, author, news agency, and topic of each.

Activity 10–7
Scavenger Hunt in the Classified Ads

Have you ever scanned the classified ads hoping to find a used car bargain or a part-time job? Perhaps you have written a classified ad of your own. Individuals who want to buy, sell, rent, or trade something can place classified ads in the newspaper. These ads produce revenue for the newspaper and serve as a clearinghouse for community commerce, as well.

Using the classified section from a newspaper, answer on a separate sheet of paper the following questions. You will need to locate and use the classified ad index to find the appropriate section for each question. Have some fun while you are on your scavenger hunt . . . some of the ads are very interesting!

1. What is the most unusual item that has been lost?

2. How many motorcycles are for sale?

3. Which used car would you buy if you had your choice?

4. Which "personal" ad do you find most interesting?

5. What job would you apply for if you were job hunting?

6. How many yard sales are listed?

7. Which two pets would you adopt if you had room in your home?

8. Which business opportunity interests you most?

9. Which number(s) would you call for a day-care center that welcomes "drop-ins"?

10. What should you do if you find an error in an ad you placed?

Activity 10–8
Writing a Classified Ad

Many people use classified ads to advertise items they would like to sell; many of these same people are surprised at the response their ads receive. A well-written classified ad can help you empty your garage and pad your wallet. To write an effective ad, there are a few basic principles you need to know, however. Above all, keep in mind that people skim ads quickly, so remember:

1. The first word of the ad should catch a reader's attention.

This	Not this
FIREWOOD, del. and stacked. Mixed pinion, oak, and pine. $72/cord. 795–6858	OLD So. Cntry. kindling, fat pine—great gifts. For free brochure write Brewton Inc. P.O. Box 555, Brewton, Pa.

2. Use as few words in the ad as possible, because the cost of placing a classified ad is determined by the length of the ad. However, you must be certain that the ad includes all necessary information.

This	Not this
1 BDRM, carpet, drapes, appls.; adults, no pets; $275 + utilities. 223–0425	CHEERFUL! Near bus, utilities, $185, 433–1064.

3. In a classified ad, abbreviations are fine—if a reader can understand them. A brief ad that makes no sense to its readers cannot be effective.

This	Not this
PENTAX C330 with 45mm, 60mm, 180mm lenses $595. Yashica with 85–250mm Zuika lens, $250. 440–1786.	PENTAX 6×7, 35, 75, 105, 135m XT, WL, EL, $1,175. Mike 623–7373.

The classified section helps you buy or sell an item or find a job.

4. Finally, be sure your ad is placed in the appropriate category in the classified ads. If you have a car to sell, place your ad in the "Automobiles for Sale" category, not "Miscellaneous."

Using the Classified Index shown on this page and keeping in mind the principles for writing good ads, compose two classified ads for things you would like to buy, sell, or rent.

```
                  CLASSIFIED INDEX

Real Estate . . . . . . . . . .1     Wanted . . . . . . . . . . . . . .8

Rentals . . . . . . . . . . . .2     Help Wanted . . . . . . . .9

Rentals Wanted . . . . . .3          Jobs Wanted . . . . . . . .10

Service Offered . . . . . .4         Lost & Found . . . . . . . .11

Household Goods . . . .5             Personals . . . . . . . . . . .12

Miscellaneous  . . . . . . .6        Motorcycles . . . . . . . . .13

Pets . . . . . . . . . . . . . .7    Automobiles . . . . . . . . .14
```

Activity 10–9
Sports Line

Thousands of avid sports fans read the sports section each day, and if you are among them you will surely enjoy this activity. Use the sports section of your newspaper to answer the questions that follow. Write your responses on a separate sheet of paper.

1. What is the headline of today's top sports story?

2. Does one sport receive more coverage today than the others? If so, what sport is it? Why do you think that sport is given more attention? Do upcoming games get more coverage than those already played?

4. What are the titles of the standings and statistics columns?

5. List all the sports in today's sports section that are given any type of coverage.

6. Did you read any articles that you thought showed the bias of the sports writer? Which team does he or she seem to prefer? How could you tell?

7. Are there any feature stories in today's sports section? If so, what topic do they discuss?

8. Is there any coverage of women's sports? If so, which ones?

9. Is there any high school sports coverage?

10. Are there any predictions of winners? If so, for which sport? List the name of the column or article in which the prediction was made.

Activity 10–10
Sports Scoreboard

In the sports section of your newspaper, you will find many tables like the one shown here. As you can see, all the teams in the National Basketball Association (NBA) are listed with their standings. There are two divisions in each conference. The conferences are divided by geographic location. This table shows wins, losses, percent of wins, and the number of games back a team is from first place. Refer to the table to answer the following questions. Write your answers on a separate sheet of paper.

1. What are the names of the two divisions in the Eastern Conference?

2. List the names of the divisions in the Western Conference.

3. Which team is in first place in each of the four divisions?

4. What statistic do the Milwaukee, New York, and Phoenix teams have in common?

5. Which four teams were "in the cellar" on the day these standings were current?

6. Which of the teams in first place looks most impressive to you? Why?

7. Which of the teams in last place looks best at this point in the season? Why?

NBA STANDINGS

EASTERN CONFERENCE
CENTRAL DIVISION

	W	L	Pct	GB
Cleveland	38	12	.760	—
Detroit	33	14	.702	3½
Milwaukee	31	17	.646	6
Atlanta	31	20	.608	7½
Bulls	29	20	.592	8½
Indiana	11	38	.224	26½

ATLANTIC DIVISION

	W	L	Pct	GB
New York	34	17	.667	—
Philadelphia	28	22	.560	5½
Boston	23	27	.460	10½
Washington	19	30	.388	14
Boston	23	27	.460	10½
Washington	19	30	.388	14
New Jersey	19	32	.373	15
Charlotte	14	37	.275	20

WESTERN CONFERENCE
MIDWEST DIVISION

	W	L	Pct	GB
Houston	31	18	.633	—
Utah	31	20	.608	1
Dallas	26	22	.542	4½
Denver	26	25	.510	6
San Antonio	13	36	.265	18
Miami	7	42	.143	24

PACIFIC DIVISION

	W	L	Pct	GB
L.A. Lakers	34	16	.680	—
Phoenix	32	17	.653	1½
Seattle	31	19	.620	3
Golden State	28	20	.583	5
Portland	25	23	.521	8
Sacramento	14	35	.286	19½
L.A. Clippers	11	40	.216	23½

Activity 10–11
Forecasting the Weather

Are you going to a football game, baseball game, track meet, or tennis match? You can use the temperatures and forecasts given in the weather section of your newspaper to help you decide what clothing to wear to be comfortable. If you are going to travel across the state, or go on a vacation to another area of the country, the weather section's predictions and present temperature lists will help you choose what to pack. The weather is a constant source of news, and the following activity will help you discover what types of weather information your newspaper provides.

Often, on the front page of a newspaper you can find a brief summary of the local weather forecast. The summary shown here is typical, giving information about the weather forecast for the day and evening.

For more detailed information, you would consult the official weather maps distributed by the U.S. Weather Bureau. These maps appear daily in most newspapers. Such things as areas of low and high atmospheric pressure, position and movements of large air masses, and storm activity are illustrated. Usually, this same information is summarized in a paragraph that you can find somewhere near the map.

Some newspapers also include information about the condition of local highways. Travelers can use this information to plan their routes.

In addition, the weather section reports on precipitation, air quality, humidity, and hourly temperatures for cities throughout the state. And if you are interested

---

Weather

DENVER AREA: Variably cloudy, not so cold and a few snow showers today. Partly cloudy, snow showers ending and cool tonight. Highs, 33-38; lows, 15-20. Details on Page 12-C.

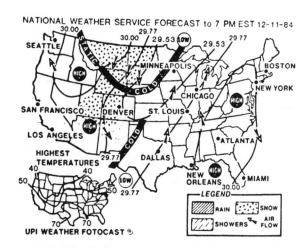

UPI WEATHER FOTOCAST ®

Cold, snow showers predicted for area

The unseasonably mild temperatures that have graced the Denver area will be replaced Tuesday by cold air and snow showers, weather forecasters said.

Ron Kelly, the Rocky Mountain News forecaster, said a storm front would move through the metropolitan area Tuesday, bringing overcast skies and rain that would change to snow in the late afternoon.

The forecast called for 1 to 2 inches of snow in the area overnight, and from 4 to 8 inches in the mountains, Kelly said. Highs for Tuesday were expected to be in the high 40s, dropping to 18 to 20 degrees Tuesday night.

Kelly said the cold weather would remain at least through Wednesday.

ROAD CONDITIONS

U.S. 6 west — Loveland Pass: icy in spots, snowpacked. I-70 west — Eisenhower Tunnel (both approaches): wet. Vail Pass: icy in spots. Glenwood Springs: icy in spots. U.S. 24 Colorado 91 — Fremont Pass: icy in spots. Tennessee Pass: wet, icy in spots. U.S. 40 west — Rabbit Ears Pass: wet, icy in spots, snowpacked in spots. Steamboat Springs: wet, icy in spots. U.S. 50 & 550 west of 285 — Monarch Pass: icy in spots. Red Mountain Pass: wet, icy in spots, snowpacked in spots. U.S. 160 west — La Veta Pass: icy in spots. Wolf Creek Pass: icy in spots, snowpacked in spots.

For updated road conditions, call the Colorado Department of Highways at 639-1111 for Denver and roads west, and 639-1234 for I-25 and roads east.

For mountain and avalanche conditions, call 236-9435 in Denver and Boulder; 482-0457 in Fort Collins, 688-5485 in Frisco, 827-5687 in Vail, and 920-1664 in Aspen.

in knowing the temperature in Tokyo, you can consult the detailed, alphabetized lists of temperatures in cities throughout the world. The U.S. Weather Bureau compiles these lists for various major cities around the globe.

Consult the charts shown, and you will see that Brownsville, Texas, and Barbados both had temperatures of 84 degrees on December 12, although one city had partly cloudy skies, while the other had clear skies. Now, try doing some more weather research on your own. Use the charts on pages 174 to 176 to answer the following questions. Write your answers on a separate sheet of paper.

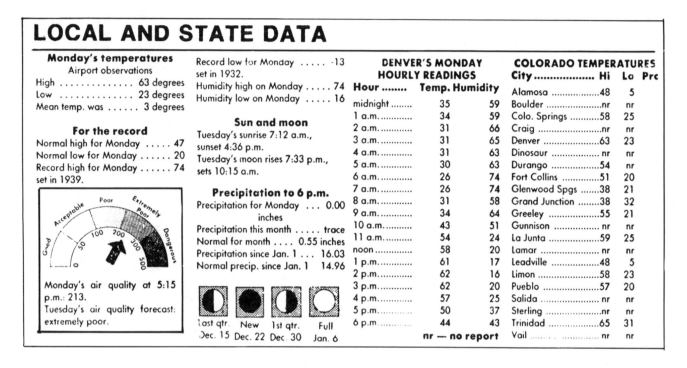

LOCAL AND STATE DATA

Monday's temperatures
Airport observations
High . . . . 63 degrees
Low . . . . 23 degrees
Mean temp. was . . . . . . 3 degrees

For the record
Normal high for Monday 47
Normal low for Monday 20
Record high for Monday 74
set in 1939.

Monday's air quality at 5:15 p.m.: 213.
Tuesday's air quality forecast: extremely poor.

Record low for Monday . . . . . -13
set in 1932.
Humidity high on Monday 74
Humidity low on Monday 16

Sun and moon
Tuesday's sunrise 7:12 a.m., sunset 4:36 p.m.
Tuesday's moon rises 7:33 p.m., sets 10:15 a.m.

Precipitation to 6 p.m.
Precipitation for Monday . . . 0.00 inches
Precipitation this month . . . . . trace
Normal for month . . . . 0.55 inches
Precipitation since Jan. 1 . . . 16.03
Normal precip. since Jan. 1 14.96

Last qtr.   New   1st qtr.   Full
Dec. 15   Dec. 22   Dec. 30   Jan. 6

DENVER'S MONDAY HOURLY READINGS

Hour	Temp.	Humidity
midnight	35	59
1 a.m.	34	59
2 a.m.	31	66
3 a.m.	31	65
4 a.m.	31	63
5 a.m.	30	63
6 a.m.	26	74
7 a.m.	26	74
8 a.m.	31	58
9 a.m.	34	64
10 a.m.	43	51
11 a.m.	54	24
noon	58	20
1 p.m.	61	17
2 p.m.	62	16
3 p.m.	62	20
4 p.m.	57	25
5 p.m.	50	37
6 p.m.	44	43

nr — no report

COLORADO TEMPERATURES

City	Hi	Lo	Prc
Alamosa	48	5	
Boulder	nr	nr	
Colo. Springs	58	25	
Craig	nr	nr	
Denver	63	23	
Dinosaur	nr	nr	
Durango	54	nr	
Fort Collins	51	20	
Glenwood Spgs	38	21	
Grand Junction	38	32	
Greeley	55	21	
Gunnison	nr	nr	
La Junta	59	25	
Lamar	nr	nr	
Leadville	48	5	
Limon	58	23	
Pueblo	57	20	
Salida	nr	nr	
Sterling	nr	nr	
Trinidad	65	31	
Vail	nr	nr	

1. What is the expected high temperature on Tuesday in the New Mexico mountains?

2. What is the expected low temperature on Tuesday in the northwest section of Kansas?

3. What was Monday's low temperature in Albany?

4. What was Monday's high temperature in Dallas/Fort Worth?

5. How much precipitation was recorded in Detroit on Monday?

6. Which two cities on the national chart recorded the lowest temperature on Monday? What was the temperature?

7. Which city on the national chart recorded the highest temperature on Monday? What was the temperature?

8. Which two cities on the foreign chart recorded the highest temperature? What was the temperature?

NATIONAL TEMPERATURES

City	Mon Dec 10				Tue Dec 11			Wed Dec 12		
	Lo	Hi	Prc	Wea	Wea	Lo	Hi	Wea	Lo	Hi
Albany	22	38	.00	Ptcldy		30	45	Ptcldy	27	48
Albuquerque ..	27	52	.00	Ptcldy		31	54	Ptcldy	34	53
Amarillo	29	66	.00	Ptcldy		29	72	Ptcldy	37	50
Atlanta	47	63	.00	Sunny		45	67	Sunny	43	68
Atlantic City ...	47	53	.00	Ptcldy		40	50	Ptcldy	37	54
Austin	51	75	.00	Ptcldy		51	77	Cloudy	53	76
Baltimore	39	50	.00	Sunny		37	53	Sunny	34	58
Billings	38	56	.00	Snow		20	35	Ptcldy	15	44
Birmingham ...	55	66	.00	Sunny		40	67	Sunny	45	70
Bismarck	19	40	.00	Windy		24	26	Ptcldy	01	28
Boise	28	42	.08	Ptcldy		27	40	Snoshw	31	40
Boston	31	49	.21	Ptcldy		40	48	Ptcldy	37	50
Brownsville	56	82	.00	Ptcldy		58	84	Ptcldy	60	84
Buffalo	36	46	.07	Ptcldy		35	48	Cloudy	39	49
Burlington Vt ..	31	40	.00	Ptcldy		29	41	Ptcldy	28	46
Casper	35	40	.00	Snow		27	39	Ptcldy	07	34
Charleston Sc ..	48	62	.00	Ptcldy		44	67	Sunny	45	71
Charleston Wv .	37	52	.41	Sunny		39	55	Sunny	34	60
Charlotte Nc ..	30	48	.06	Sunny		36	60	Sunny	35	66
Cheyenne	23	55	.00	Cloudy		25	45	Cloudy	11	35
Chicago	33	46	.08	Sunny		31	55	Cloudy	32	32
Cincinnati	45	50	.13	Sunny		38	51	Cloudy	38	55
Cleveland	36	41	.22	Sunny		36	48	Ptcldy	36	52
Columbia Sc...	31	62	.00	Ptcldy		39	68	Sunny	40	72
Columbus Oh ..	39	44	.38	Sunny		37	50	Ptcldy	37	54
Dal Ft Worth ..	43	71	.00	Sunny		47	72	Cloudy	54	69
Denver	23	63	.00	Snoshw		30	50	Ptcldy	20	40
Des Moines....	29	45	.00	Ptcldy		32	57	Cloudy	19	28
Detroit	30	46	.12	Sunny		33	46	Cloudy	32	42
Duluth........	30	34	.00	Cloudy		30	37	Sunny	06	15
El Paso	31	66	.00	Ptcldy		33	70	Ptcldy	37	69
Fargo	23	37	.00	Windy		26	28	Ptcldy	01	21
Flagstaff	19	18	.00	Snow		30	39	Ptcldy	20	47
Great Falls	42	53	.00	Snoshw		16	32	Windy	20	46

FORECAST FOR THE REGION

New Mexico — Variable clouds Tuesday and Tuesday night, chance of showers and mountain snow showers mainly west and north. Highs Tuesday, 40 to 50 mountains and northwest. 50s to mid-70s lower elevations. Lows, teens to 20s mountains, mid-20s to near 40 lower elevations.

Kansas — Partly cloudy and mild Tuesday. Mostly cloudy Tuesday night, chance of light snow northwest and north-central. Highs

Tuesday, mid-50s to mid-60s statewide. Lows, low 20s northwest, mid-30s east.

Utah — Mostly cloudy north Tuesday, scattered rain and snow showers, variable clouds south both days, widely scattered showers. Locally gusty winds statewide Tuesday. Highs Tuesday, mid-30s to mid-40s north, 40s south. Lows, low 20s-low 30s north, low 20s to mid-30s south.

Nebraska — Considerable clouds and colder Tuesday, increasing winds in afternoon, slight chance of showers west and north.

FOREIGN CITIES

City	Hi	Lo	Wth	City	Hi	Lo	Wth
Acapulco	90	75	cdy	London	48	41	clr
Amsterdam	50	46	clr	Madrid	57	43	clr
Athens	63	41	clr	Mazatlan	87	71	cdy
Barbados	84	72	clr	Manila	88	66	clr
Berlin	45	37	cdy	Merida/Cancun	84	57	clr
B'Aires	77	61	cdy	Mexico City	73	46	clr
Cairo	66	48	clr	Montreal	39	32	cdy
Calgary	39	18	cdy	Moscow	36	34	sn
Copenhagen	49	41	clr	New Delhi	81	52	clr
Dublin	52	39	clr	Ottawa	34	1	cdy
Edmonton	32	0	clr	Paris	48	45	clr
Frankfurt	46	32	cdy	Regina	24	-4	cdy
Geneva	39	32	cdy	Rome	55	34	clr
Guadalajara	80	41	clr	San Juan	72	70	cdy
Hong Kong	73	64	clr	Stockholm	45	37	clr
Jerusalem	54	39	cdy	Tokyo	57	43	cdy
Kingston	90	73	cdy	Toronto	39	32	cdy
				Vancouver	43	36	rn
				Vienna	39	32	cdy

9. What kind of weather is predicted for Denver?

10. What was the record low for Denver on December 11th? (Hint: It was set in 1932.)

Activity 10–12
Understanding Stock Quotations

Every day, you can read in your newspaper about the stock market. Why is stock market activity such important news? Because the buying and selling that happens on Wall Street affects many individuals' incomes, as well as the economies of the United States and the world. Perhaps you have invested in stocks yourself. If so, you probably turn quickly to the stock quotations whenever you pick up a newspaper.

If you do not yet know how to read stock quotations, you are about to enter the world of Wall Street. To read and understand the stock exchange pages found in the business sections of all metropolitan papers, you must first learn some essen-

tial terms. On a separate sheet of paper, take notes on these terms and their definitions.

Year's high: the highest price the stock reached in one year's time.

Year's low: the lowest price the stock reached in one year's time.

Day's high: the highest price the stock reached on a given day.

Day's low: the lowest price the stock reached on a given day.

Last price: the price at which the stock was selling when the market closed for the day.

Net change: the difference between a stock's last price today and the same stock's last price on the previous day of trading.

NYSE: New York Stock Exchange: one of the major stock exchanges.

⅞ = 87.5 cents

¾ = 75.0 cents

⅝ = 62.5 cents

½ = 50.0 cents

⅜ = 37.5 cents

¼ = 25.0 cents

⅛ = 12.5 cents

Now, look at the stock quotations that follow and answer questions one to four. Use the terminology you just learned to find the answers.

52-week High	Low	Stock	Div.	Yld.	PE	100s	Sales High	Low	Last	Chg.
13⅝	4⅞	Mattel					11½	11¼	11¼	−¼
32⅞	23	Goodyr					25	24½	24½	
33¾	20¼	Chryslr					27½	26½	27¼	−⅜

1. What were the year's high, year's low, day's high, day's low, last price, and net change for Chrysler stock?

2. Using the stock quotations for Goodyear, provide the same information requested in Question 1.

3. Using the stock quotations for Mattel, provide the same information requested in Question 1.

4. Finally, survey the stock quotations for several companies whose names are familiar to you. Using a metropolitan newspaper, look up the year's high, year's low, day's high, day's low, last price, and net change for the following stocks: Alcoa, Campbell's Soup, Delta Air Lines, Exxon, and K Mart.

Activity 10–13
Stock Quotation Worksheet

Are you a Wall Street wizard? Using the New York Stock Exchange (NYSE) quotations from a metropolitan paper, look up the following stocks and, on a separate sheet of paper, record these statistics for each stock listed below: the abbreviation for the stock, year's high, year's low, day's high, day's low, last price, and net change.

Ford Motor Company	Kellogg's	Texas Instruments
General Electric	Penney's	United Air Lines
Honda	PepsiCo	Wendys
Motorola	Scott Paper	Xerox

After you find all the information requested above, answer the following questions:

1. Which of the stocks has the highest *last* price per share?

2. What was that stock's *last* price?

3. Which of the stocks has the lowest *last* price per share?

4. What was that stock's *last* price?

5. Which stock recorded the largest *net gain* from the previous day?

6. How much did that stock gain?

7. Which stock recorded the largest *net loss* from the previous day?

8. How much was that stock down?

9. If you were buying one of these twelve stocks, which would you buy? Why?

The business section contains stock prices and news about companies.

Activity 10–14
Magazine Preferences

Reading for pleasure certainly must include magazines. You may particularly enjoy browsing through a favorite magazine relating to a hobby or sport or cars or fashion. Some magazines are funny or inspirational; some magazines are interesting and informative. No matter what your reason for reading a specific magazine, you need to recognize that reading magazines is an important part of reading for pleasure.

And reading for enjoyment is important for developing reading speed, reading comprehension, and vocabulary. The more you read, the more practice you have improving your reading skills, the more contact you have with words and word meanings, and the more your reading speed improves. Although reading a magazine may seem like nothing but pure enjoyment, you benefit by doing it.

Let's begin by surveying your magazine reading habits. On a separate sheet of paper, number from one to five, skipping every other line. Answer the following questions regarding your leisure reading preferences.

1. Which magazine(s) do you enjoy reading most? Why?

2. Do you read the entire magazine, or do you read only parts of it? If you read only parts of it, which parts do you read?

3. Do you read entire articles in the magazine, or do you simply skim them? Why?

4. Where and when do you read magazines? Why do you choose this time and location?

5. Do you enjoy reading magazines more than reading books? Why?

Activity 10–15
Magazine Survey

There are hundreds of magazines on newsstands and library shelves today. Select a magazine you have never read before and skim through it. Choose an article that catches your interest or makes you curious and read it. Next, using a separate sheet of paper, write down the name of the magazine you selected and the title of the article you read. Then briefly state the article's main idea. Do the same survey with a second magazine and, if you have time, a third magazine, as well. (Remember, don't be tempted by your usual favorites—choose a magazine that's new to you to explore.) Be prepared to explain why you selected the magazines you did and to discuss whether you would like to continue to read those titles.

Activity 10–16
Magazine Summary

Bring to class a magazine you enjoy reading. Choose an article and, simply for pleasure, read it. Now, on a separate sheet of paper, write a short paragraph summarizing the gist of the article.

You are certain to find at least one magazine you will enjoy reading from the variety available.

Was reading and summarizing easy or difficult for you? If it was easy, you are comprehending well enough during leisure reading to get the main idea of the content. Did you find yourself skimming the article, selectively skipping sentences or sections you did not enjoy, or did you read the article word for word? Were you still able to get the gist of the article using the skimming and skipping reading technique?

You do not have to feel guilty skimming or selectively skipping passages as you read for pleasure. After all, you are not reading for specific details; you are not going to be tested on the material. Reading for pleasure in your leisure time should be enjoyable!

Repeat this activity frequently. On a separate sheet of paper prepare a chart like the one shown. Each time you complete the exercise, log it on your chart.

Name of magazine	Title of article	Summary
1.		
2.		

Activity 10–17
Selecting an Enjoyable Book

Have you read any good books lately? For some people, sitting back and getting lost in a good book is the most relaxing thing they can do.

Rediscover the joy of reading a book for pleasure. Your instructor will set aside some class time for leisure reading. Your task is to choose a book to read—

one that you will enjoy. If you start a book and don't like it, select another. It defeats the purpose of this activity to have you suffer through a book you don't like.

The first step, then, is to find a book you will enjoy. You might ask your librarian to suggest some books other students have liked. Or, your instructor may have some ideas that interest you. On the other hand, you may prefer to browse independently, skimming covers and summaries to find a book that suits you. However you go about finding your books, enjoy this opportunity to get reacquainted with reading for pleasure.

Activity 10–18
Reading for Pleasure

To get a good start on reading the book you have selected, your instructor will set aside some class time. So you can keep a record of your reading progress, on a separate sheet of paper make a chart like the one that follows. Each time you read your book, log on your chart the date and the number of pages you read.

Remember, as you read, your reading speed is increasing, your comprehension is improving, and your vocabulary is growing. Not bad, since reading a book you enjoy is a pleasure, anyway!

	Date	Number of pages read		Date	Number of pages read
1			4		
2			5		
3			6		

Activity 10–19
Creative Book Projects[1]

If your instructor says *book report*, she or he is likely to hear a loud groan in response. This activity gives you the opportunity to do something much more creative and fun than writing a typical book report. From the list that follows, choose the format for a creative book project that appeals to you. Be sure to include your book's title and author somewhere in your project.

1. Create a crossword puzzle based on your book. Include at least forty *Across* clues and forty *Down* clues and make certain that most of your clues are related directly to your book. The only exceptions to this rule are words or definitions that you have to use as "fillers." Include a key for the crossword puzzle.

[1]The suggestions in this activity are taken from Isabelle M. Decker, *100 Novel Ways with Book Reports*. New York: Scholastic Magazines, Inc., 1969.

2. Construct an exam of at least fifty questions based on your book. Include multiple-choice, matching, true–false, and completion questions on your exam. Try to use approximately the same number of each type of question. You may include other kinds of questions, such as short essays, but provide an outline of possible essay answers along with an answer key for the objective questions.

3. Design an oversized poster based on your book. Include in the design a 300-word recommendation "advertising" the book. This format lends itself very well to sports stories and mysteries.

4. Draw a detailed map of the book's primary setting and then explain in sequence the important action that occurred at the various places illustrated on your map. Completeness, creativity, and neatness are important here.

5. Choose either a major or minor character from your book and explain his or her part in the plot or sequence of events. Then, explain how you would have reacted or behaved differently.

6. You are a literary critic. Choose one of the following and discuss the statement, reflecting and amplifying on your book.
    A. "Authors are people behind masks."
    B. "The biographer is a maker of heels or heroes."
    C. "Show me what the age is reading, and I can tell you the nature of the times."
    D. "This book should be included in a capsule buried today, to be dug up in 100 years."
    E. "This book should be read by every young adult and his or her parents."

7. Condense the action in your book into various articles and present them as though they made up the front page of a newspaper. Use a standard six-column newspaper format. Include human interest stories, sports events, obituaries, editorials, want ads, advertising, and so on. Make sure all of your articles reflect the book you read and the era in which its story action took place. (For example, Tom Sawyer would not be riding a ten-speed racing bicycle.)

8. Write a television commercial about your book. Include all necessary dialogue, as well as descriptions of the story action. Draw pictures or use magazine illustrations to convey your ideas. The illustrations should reveal what your commercial would look like if shown on television.

9. If you chose to read a collection of short stories, you may wish to do one of the following:
    A. Write your intellectual reactions to five stories, rather than analyzing them. Discuss the type of reader who would enjoy or find satisfaction in reading each story. To justify your position, present at least three positive aspects of a story you liked and three negative aspects of one you disliked.
    B. Write an essay on the significance and importance of titles, referring to the titles of ten specific stories to support your generalizations.

Activity 10–20
Traditional Book Projects

Some students feel more confident following a more conventional form for a book project, and some books lend themselves to this type of report format. If you are one of this group, or if you feel that the book you chose fits the traditional project category, try the following:

1. In the center of the page on a separate sheet of paper, write the title of the book you read and underline it. Beneath the title, write the author's name.

2. For Part One of your report, begin by describing the action in the book. In other words, what was the plot of the story?

Choose three of the following to conclude your book project.

3. Describe in detail the main character of the book you read. Include a description of his or her appearance, personality, motivations, and so on. Point out whether this character changed through the course of the story.

4. Describe what you consider the climax of the plot and tell why.

5. Discuss whether you think the book is true to life and, if not, why.

6. Tell about the incident or aspect of the book that you either really liked or really disliked.

7. Give your general evaluation of the book, including what you liked and disliked about it. Would you recommend it to anyone else?

Activity 10–21
Unit Review

Number a separate sheet of paper from one through twenty-five. Read the questions below and write the correct answers beside the corresponding numbers on your answer sheet.

I. Sections of the Newspaper
Identify the section of the newspaper being described by writing the name of the section in the corresponding space on your answer sheet.

1. The _____ section deals with entertainment. It includes information about movies, plays, concerts, and nightlife. It also includes the comics.

2. This section is essential for the paper because it provides the money to publish the paper. It is called the _____ section.

3. The _____ is what the reader sees first. It influences his or her decision about whether to buy the paper.

4. _____ focus on individuals who have died and give accounts of occupation, relatives, funeral information, and so on.

5. The _____ section focuses on opinions of staff writers, the general public, and syndicated columnists.

6. The previous night's basketball game, the top sports statistics, and news of a player trade are covered in the _____ section.

7. Stock quotations are found in the _____ section, along with articles on new products, marketing strategies, and companies of note.

II. Newspaper Jargon
Match the terms given with their correct definitions.

8. Banner headline	A. Continued on page _____
9. Headline	B. The first paragraph of a story
10. Byline	C. Associated Press
11. News agency	D. The line indicating who wrote the article
12. A.P.	
13. U.P.I.	E. Words beside or below a photograph or illustration
14. Lead	F. United Press International
15. Caption	G. An organization that sends news stories by wire
16. Jump	H. Large type above an article indicating the content of the article
	I. A headline that stretches from one side of the newspaper page to the other

III. Business and Financial Section
Study the stock quotation given below and identify each numbered section with the term that describes it.

17.	18.	19.	20.	21.	22.	23.
13⅞	4⅞	Mattel	11½	11¼	11½	−¼

IV. Classified Ads
Since you pay for Classified Ads by the word, it is to your advantage to use as few words in an ad as possible. Rewrite the classified ad below, making it brief, yet complete. (Hint: thirty-five to forty words will supply all the necessary information.)

24. FOR SALE—I would like to sell for $75 the Victorian sofa my husband says is like new. I also have a dining room table and four chairs for $160 that I really want to get rid of. Because we have a new color TV set, I will also sell my 7-year-old portable TV for $24. Last year we bought a new G.E. Electric range for $750, but I really don't like it. I will be willing to let it go for $300. Anyone who is interested in any of these terrific bargains should call me at 123–4567. But be sure not to call until after 5:00 P.M. because I won't be home from work until then.

V. Reading for Pleasure
No matter what you prefer to read—newspapers, magazines, or books—reading for pleasure is good for you.

25. In a short essay explain the benefits of reading for pleasure.

UNIT ELEVEN

Summing It Up

SUMMING UP (sŭm'ming ŭp) v. to summarize

*T*his is the final unit in your student worktext. Take a moment to consider what you have learned. Think about changes you've made in your study setting, your study techniques, your test-taking strategies, and your note-taking methods. Have your reading speed and comprehension improved? What do you know about the dictionary, the newspaper, and the library that you did not know before?

To assess your progress, you'll need to answer all these questions; this unit will help you accomplish that. In addition, you'll understand that the skills you learned in this worktext will benefit you not only in other classes, but throughout your life. Even after you leave school, you will be reading and learning. You must continue to do both in order to adapt to and live in our ever changing world.

Activity 11–1
Preparing for the Worktext Review

To assess your progress, we'll begin by evaluating how much *information* and *knowledge* you have gained in the areas mentioned in the unit introduction. You will need to study and prepare for a worktext review, which will be similar to the unit reviews with which you are already familiar. To help you get ready:

1. Begin by creating a good study setting for yourself. (See Unit 2 to review what a good study setting consists of.)

2. Create a budget for your time; allow enough time in the day over several days for proper review of the material. (See Unit 2 for tips on budgeting your time.)

3. Review your text using the techniques described in Unit 2, "Previewing Your Text," to refresh your memory on the information this worktext covers.

4. Review your notes. Begin by using a highlighter to mark important material you anticipate will be covered on the review. Write margin notes identifying main points. Then, look at your margin notes and recite the material to be learned. (See Unit 3—"Note Taking.")

5. Remember, you should study for brief periods each day over several days; your memory will absorb the material and give you reliable recall if you study that way. (See Unit 4—"Taking Tests.")

6. Prepare for your review using the techniques listed in Activity 4–3 in Unit 4.

7. Assess your anxiety and practice the techniques that work for you. You'll find suggestions in Unit 4, Activity 4–4, to help you control your anxiety.

8. Finally, when you do the worktext review, use the techniques outlined in Unit 4, Activities 4–5 through 4–7, to achieve the best possible results.

Material to Cover

Unit 2: Developing Study Skills

Previewing your textbook: What is involved? Why do it? What are the seven steps in the process?

Study setting: List seven tips.

Budgeting time: What should a time budget include, and how do you make one up?

Study sequence: What three choices do you have?

SQ3R: Describe the process by explaining what each letter and number stands for.

Sizing up your instructor: Explain the steps and the benefits of sizing up your instructor.

Unit 3: Note Taking

Methods of note taking: List five methods and draw an illustration or write an explanation for each.

Shortcuts: List five shortcuts and give two examples of each.

Unit 4: Taking Tests

Memory: Explain the four layers of memory, what happens in each layer, and how you prepare for each.

Preparing for a test: List the steps.

Relieving anxiety: List tips that work for you.

Test-taking strategies: List the steps.

Test-taking tricks: List tips for answering true–false, multiple-choice, matching, and completion questions.

Test terminology: Explain what is required for each of the twelve test terms listed in the unit.

Unit 5: Improving Your Understanding

Define and be able to apply the following:

main idea	comprehension	cause and effect
gist	sequence	inference
key words	cloze	predicting

Unit 6: Increasing Speed

What three factors determine reading speed?

List five ways to build a good vocabulary.

Describe how your eyes move when you read; explain what happens when your eyes fixate.

Discuss four common reading problems and one way to correct each.

Unit 7: Skimming and Scanning

Define and explain when to use:

skimming	review	average rate
scanning	overview	rapid rate
preview	study rate	very rapid rate
	slow and careful rate	

What three factors determine reading rate?

What two factors determine the ability to read fast?

Unit 8: Using the Dictionary
Define and be able to identify:

main entry	guide words
etymology	homograph
syllabication	diacritical marks
variants	parts of speech
inflected forms	

Unit 10: Reading for Enjoyment
Define and be able to identify:

byline	net change	day's low
dateline	headline	two national news agencies
caption	banner headline	editorial
jump	year's high	news story
lead	year's low	two stock exchanges
last price	day's high	five Ws

Be able to recognize the type of story found in the business section, editorial section, sports section, and feature section.

Be able to read stock market quotation sheets.

Know the four criteria of a good classified ad.

Activity 11–2
Worktext Review

Number a separate sheet of paper from 1 to 133. This activity will assess your comprehension of the material and activities in this worktext.

I. Study Skills: Previewing Your Text

1 to 7. Skim the following seven steps in previewing a text and decide in what order they should be done. Place the letter of the step that should be done first beside number one on your paper, the letter of the step that should be done second beside number two, and so on.

A. Page through the book and look at the charts, pictures, graphs, and so on.

B. Look at the appendixes (glossary, index, and so on).

C. Skim the table of contents.

D. Evaluate the difficulty of the material.

E. Look at the title, author, and date of publication.

F. Know your purpose for reading the text.

G. Read the preface or introduction.

8. Why is it important to preview your text? Place the letter of the correct answer beside number eight on your paper.
   A. To become acquainted with the material to be covered in class before the class actually begins
   B. To determine how difficult the material will be for you
   C. To explore the type of information, study aids, and so on available in the text before actually using it
   D. All of the above

Study Skills: Note Taking

Write *True* if the statement is true and *False* if the statement is false beside the appropriate number on your paper.

9. The *outline* system of note taking consists of Roman numerals followed by capital letters, numbers, small letters, and so on.

10. The *listing* system of note taking resembles a diagram or a pattern, the shape of which is determined by the information.

11. Signal words point you to important information in a text. *Full signals* are words such as *next, then, last,* and *moreover.*

12. *Half signals* are words such as *first, second,* and *third.*

13. One shortcut in note taking is the *no vowel* technique. It involves leaving the last letter, if it is a vowel, off the word.

14. A useful shortcut in note taking is using *technical symbols.* An example of this would be using = in place of the word *equals.*

15. A note-taking shortcut is to use the beginning of a word in place of the entire word. An example is *Intro* for the word *Introduction.*

Study Skills: Study Setting

There are several ways to improve concentration while studying, and these involve the study setting. For example, if you *study in the same place each day,* concentration improves.

16 to 20. List five other tips for improving study setting.

Study Skills: Additional Material

21. There are three choices for determining the order in which you should study subjects. Which *is not* a correct study sequence?

A. Easiest to hardest

B. Hardest to easiest

C. Mmost important to least important

D. Alternating activities

22 to 26. Explain what each of the letters stands for in *SQ3R*.

Study Skills: Taking Tests

27 to 30. Explain the four layers of memory, what happens in each, and how you prepare for each.

31 to 35. List five methods for relieving text anxiety that work for you.

Match the following descriptions with the test terminologies they describe. Place the letter of the correct answer beside the proper number on your answer sheet.

36. Give your own judgment or opinion based on reasons; good and bad points should be included.

37. Give details, progress, or history of the topic from beginning to end.

38. Include a chart, graph, or drawing with labels and a brief explanation if needed.

39. Give both similarities and differences.

40. Give differences only.

A. contrast

B. trace

C. diagram

D. criticize

E. compare

Choose the letter of the answer that *is not* a trick for the type of test given, and write the letter beside the appropriate number on your paper.

41. On a *true–false* test:

A. Beware of qualifying words such as *all, none,* and *never,* which usually make the statement false.

B. Beware of qualifying words such as *usually, sometimes,* and *generally,* which usually make the statement true.

C. Watch for four *true* or *false* responses in a row; the next response will always be the opposite of the previous four.

D. Be aware of false logic that makes the statement false.

42. On a *multiple-choice* test:

   A. Watch for patterns in the answers, such as *A, A, B, A, A, B*.

   B. Look for the longest answer; it is frequently the correct one.

   C. Pay attention to "all of the above"; it is frequently the correct response.

   D. Eliminate first the answer that is obviously incorrect.

43. On a *matching* test:

   A. Read the list on the right first.

   B. Read the list on the left first.

   C. Read the entire list of choices, because an answer may appear to be correct, but a more correct answer might appear farther down the list.

   D. Answer the questions you are sure of first, and use the process of elimination to answer those you are unsure of.

44. On a *completion* test:

   A. Read the question several times; the key word to complete the statement may pop into your head.

   B. Look for context clues within the question that may provide you with the correct answer.

   C. Look for *a* or *an*; *a* will be followed by an answer beginning with a consonant and *an* will be followed by an answer beginning with a vowel.

   D. Never go by first instinct on completion; give the question a lot of thought, and leave it blank if you don't know the answer.

45. On an *essay* test:

   A. Plan your time carefully.

   B. Never write the outline for your essay answer on the paper; the instructor might think you are cheating.

   C. Understand the test terminology; if you are asked to *compare*, make sure you list similarities and differences.

   D. Write neatly, leave suitable margins, and allow space between answers.

46. In preparing for a test:

   A. Anticipate what material might be on the test.

   B. Reread the entire text material thoroughly.

   C. Find out what type of questions might be on the test so you can use the appropriate study techniques.

   D. Discover how much material is based on your notes.

47. In preparing for a test:

    A. Skim the material on the first night.

    B. Skim the material, look at margin notes, and recite aloud on the second night.

    C. Look at your margin notes and recite important points on the third night.

    D. Take a break on the fourth night.

48. The day of the test:

    A. Eat a small breakfast so you don't upset your stomach; coffee and donuts are good.

    B. Get your mind and body stimulated with exercise.

    C. Wear something comfortable that makes you feel confident.

    D. Build your self-confidence.

49. When taking any test:

    A. Arrive early in order to compose yourself.

    B. Bring all materials with you.

    C. Sit by a friend; it will make you feel better.

    D. Listen carefully to the instructor's directions.

50. When taking any test:

    A. Begin with the first question and work through the test in the order the questions appear.

    B. Answer the easy questions first to build your confidence.

    C. Answer objective questions before essay questions; they may provide you with responses for the essay.

    D. Guess at the answers you don't know, unless there is a penalty for guessing.

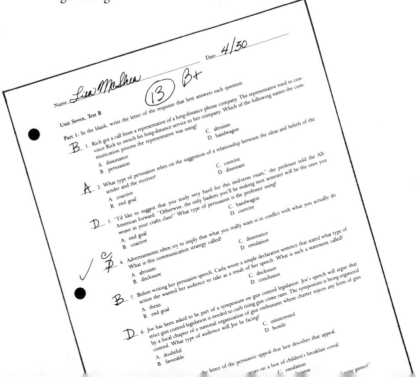

II. Comprehension
Match the following descriptions with the terms that identify them. Place the letter of the correct answer beside the corresponding number on your answer sheet.

51. the point the author is trying to make

52. an exercise in which you bring closure to a statement by supplying the missing word

53. understanding the point(s) the author is trying to make

54. putting things in order

55. meaning is not clearly stated; you must look at clues to gain it by _____

56. what happens next is not clearly stated; you must _____ it

A. inference

B. predicting

C. cloze

D. main idea

E. sequence

F. comprehension

III. Increasing Speed
Determine which answer fits the blank in the statement and write that answer beside the corresponding number on your answer sheet.

Three things determine your reading speed. They are ____57____, ____58____, and ____59____.

Two factors influence your ability to read material rapidly. They are ____60____ and ____61____.

The best readers know reading rates are ____62____; they know you do not read everything at the same ____63____.

When you read, your eyes make an ____64____ rather than moving in a straight line.

When you read, your eyes pause or stop to take in words; this pause or stop is called a ____65____.

____66____ is saying words aloud as you read them; it slows down reading speed.

67 to 71. Improving your vocabulary will improve your reading speed. List five ways to improve your vocabulary.

IV. Skimming and Scanning
    Place the letter of the correct definition for the term given beside the
    corresponding number on your answer sheet.

72. skimming

73. scanning

74. preview

75. review

76. overview

77. average rate

78. study rate

A. used when reading for pleasure

B. follows a previous reading; it is used to go back over material

C. quickly passing over the entire selection to get the gist of it

D. an end in itself; it gives you an overall impression of the material

E. looking over material rapidly to find a specific piece of information; then reading stops

F. followed by a second, more thorough reading

G. the slowest rate; it is used for difficult material and provides a high degree of understanding

V. Using the Dictionary
   Place the letter of the correct definition for the term given beside the
   corresponding number on your answer sheet.

79. main entry

80. etymology

81. syllabication

82. variants

83. inflected forms

84. homograph

85. diacritical marks

86. guide words

87. parts of speech

A. pronunciation marks

B. spellings that are irregular

C. the history or origin of a word

D. the word you are looking up

E. found in italics following the word you are looking up

F. words that are spelled the same, but have different meanings or origins

G. division of a word into syllables

H. the first and last words on a page; these words are found at the top of a dictionary

I. two or more spellings of the same word

J. none of the above

Consult the dictionary entries provided. Write the answer to the question beside the corresponding number on your paper.

88. What are the two guide words for this page?

89. Give the etymology of the word *camouflage*.

90. What is the etymological meaning of the word *camouflage?*

91. What is the syllabication of the word *camouflage?*

92. What is the variant spelling of the word *camomile?*

93. Give the inflected form of the word *canary*.

94. There is a set of homographs in these entries. Write the words that are homographs.

95. Which homograph entry is more commonly used by all of us?

96. Write the word *campaign*, including its diacritical marks.

97. Give all the parts of speech of the word *campaign*.

---

camisole | candescent

The operator of a motion-picture or television camera.

cam·i·sole (kăm'ĭ-sōl') *n.* A woman's short, sleeveless undergarment. [< LLat. *camisia*, shirt.]

cam·o·mile (kăm'ə-mīl') *n.* Var. of **chamomile.**

cam·ou·flage (kăm'ə-fläzh', -fläj') *n.* A means of concealment that creates the effect of being part of the natural surroundings. —*v.* **-flaged, -flag·ing.** To conceal by such means. [< Ital. *camuffare*, to disguise.] —**cam'ou·flag'er** *n.*

camp¹ (kămp) *n.* **1. a.** A place where a group of persons is temporarily lodged in makeshift shelters. **b.** The shelters in such a place or the persons using them. **2.** A place consisting of more or less permanent vacation cabins. **3.** A group favorable to a common cause, doctrine, or political system. —*v.* To shelter or lodge in a camp; encamp. [< Lat. *campus*, field.]

camp² (kămp) *n.* Artificiality of manner or style, appreciated for its humor, triteness, or vulgarity. —*adj.* Having the qualities of such a manner or style: *a camp movie.* [Orig. unknown.] —**camp'i·ly** *adv.* —**camp'i·ness** *n.* —**camp'y** *adj.*

cam·paign (kăm-pān') *n.* **1.** A series of military operations undertaken to achieve a specific objective within a given area. **2.** An organized activity or operation to attain a political, social, or commercial goal. —*v.* To engage in a campaign. [< OItal. *campagna*, battlefield.] —**cam·paign'er** *n.*

cam·pa·ni·le (kăm'pə-nē'lē) *n.* A bell tower, esp. one near but not attached to a church. [Ital.]

camp·er (kăm'pər) *n.* **1.** A person who camps outdoors or who attends a camp. **2. a.** A vehicle resembling an automobile-and-trailer combination, designed to serve as a dwelling and used for camping or long motor trips.

be excused? Yes, you can. [< OE *cunnan*, to know how.]

Usage: In speech *can* is used more frequently than *may* to express permission, even though traditionalists insist that *can* should be used only to express the capacity to do something. Technically, correct usage therefore requires: *May I have the car tonight?* Because the contraction *mayn't* is felt to be stilted, however, the negative form of this question is usually expressed as *Can't I have the car tonight?*

can² (kăn) *n.* **1.** A metal container. **2. a.** An airtight storage container usu. made of tincoated iron. **b.** The amount that a can holds. —*v.* **canned, can·ning. 1.** To seal in a can or jar. **2.** *Slang.* **a.** To dismiss; fire. **b.** To dispense with: *can the chatter.* [< OE *canne*, water container.] —**can'ner** *n.*

Canada goose *n.* A common wild goose of North America, with grayish plumage, a black neck and head, and a white face patch.

Ca·na·di·an French (kə-nā'dē-ən) *n.* French as used in Canada.

ca·naille (kə-nī', -nāl') *n.* The common people. [< Ital. *canaglia.*]

ca·nal (kə-năl') *n.* **1.** A man-made waterway. **2.** *Anat.* A tube or duct. [< Lat. *canalis*, channel.] —**ca·nal·i·za'tion** *n.* —**ca·nal·ize'** *v.*

can·a·pé (kăn'ə-pā', -pē) *n.* A cracker or small, thin piece of bread or toast topped with a spread or a tidbit, and served as an appetizer. [Fr.]

ca·nard (kə-närd') *n.* A false or unfounded story. [Fr.]

ca·nary (kə-nâr'ē) *n., pl.* **-ies.** A usu. yellow songbird popular as a cage bird. [< the *Canary* Islands.] —**ca·nary** *adj.*

ca·nas·ta (kə-năs'tə) *n.* A card game related to rummy and requiring two decks of cards. [Sp.]

VI. Reading for Enjoyment—Newspaper Terms

Choose the term(s) at the right that best fit(s) the sentence and place the letter(s) beside the corresponding number on your answer sheet.

98 and 99. The two national news agencies that provide stories for newspapers across the country are called _____ and _____.

100. A _____ tells the author of the article.

101. A _____ tells where the story takes place.

102. The _____ consists of words under a photograph or illustration giving information about it.

103. A line stating that a story is continued on another page is called the _____.

104. The line in bold print above a story telling briefly what the story is about is called the _____.

105. A headline that stretches across the newspaper page from one side to the other is called a _____.

106. The first paragraph of a story is called the _____.

107. Articles expressing opinions are called _____.

108. The name of a major stock exchange is the _____.

109. The highest price a stock reached in a year's time is called the _____.

110. The lowest price a stock sold for in a year's time is called the _____.

111. The highest price a stock sold for on a given day is called the _____.

112. The lowest price a stock sold for on a given day is called the _____.

113. The price a stock was selling for when the market closed for the day is called the _____.

114. The difference between today's closing price and the previous day's closing price is called the _____.

A. New York Stock Exchange

B. headline

C. last price

D. day's high

E. year's high

F. jump

G. caption

H. Associated Press

I. byline

J. editorials

K. day's low

L. United Press International

M. dateline

N. year's low

O. banner headline

P. lead

Q. net change

Leads

Each sentence listed below represents the lead of a front page story, feature story, sports story, or editorial. Beside the appropriate number on your answer sheet, write the letter of the section in which the lead would be found.

A. Front page   C. Sports section
B. Feature section   D. Editorial section

115. To the delight of area fishermen, the State Department of Conservation released 5,000 two-pound bass in Lake Neoga today.

116. Five passengers in a convertible were injured seriously today in a three-car crash on Route 88.

117. The time has come for the United States government to take a long hard look at its tariff laws.

118. Everyone who saw the long-awaited showing of *Breakfast in Berlin* last night witnessed a first in film history.

119. A missed seven-foot putt almost cost Don Sawyer the top prize in the Coles County Open on Sunday.

120. This newspaper feels that the best qualified candidate for governor is Nick Donley.

STOCK QUOTATIONS				
Stocks				
AT&T	48¾	47½	48¾	+ ⅞
Campbell's Soup	32¾	30½	32¾	+1¾
Eastman Kodak	71½	69½	71¼	+1½
Holiday Inn	39½	39½	39½	. . . .
Motorola	73	72	72¼	− ¾
Sears Roebuck	15⅝	15⅛	15½	+ ¼
Coca-Cola	34⅛	33½	33⅞	+ ½
Dan River	15⅛	14⅞	15⅛	+ ⅜

Using the stock market quotations shown, determine the correct answer and write it beside the corresponding number on your answer sheet.

121. Which stock costs the most per share?

122. What is that stock's closing price?

123. Which stock costs the least per share?

124. What is that stock's closing price?

125. Which stock recorded the greatest gain from the previous day?

126. How much did that stock gain?

127. Which stock recorded the greatest loss from the previous day?

128. How much did that stock lose?

129. Which stock was unchanged from the previous day?

Classified Ads

130 to 133. List the four criteria used in writing a good classified ad.

VII. Essay
What was the most valuable skill you learned in this class? Why? (Explain in a short paragraph.)

Activity 11–3
Reading Progress Assessment

Now that you have been able to assess what you have gained from the worktext, you can continue by considering the progress you made in reading skills. Again, don't become anxious—this is not a test you could or should have studied for. No one fails an assessment. Instead, it's hoped you will be pleased with your results and your progress.

Activity 11–4
Progress Chart

So that you have a composite picture of how your skills have improved and your speeds increased, on a separate sheet of paper, create a chart resembling the one that follows. Next, begin by turning back to your Rapid Discrimination Drills chart. Record your fastest speed and your slowest speed; determine your progress by subtracting the slower figure from the faster one.

Turn now to your Comprehension Activities chart and make the same calculation. Follow that with calculations for Speed-reading Activities (if you did them). Finally, record the information from your Assessment Test.

Now look at the total picture. How did you do?

PROGRESS CHART

Rapid Discrimination Drills

Fastest Speed _____

Slowest Speed _____

Progress _____

Comprehension Activities

Fastest Speed _____

Slowest Speed _____

Progress _____

Speed-reading Drills

Fastest Speed _____

Slowest Speed _____

Progress _____

Assessment Test

Level at which you last tested: Comprehension _____ Vocabulary _____

Level at which you first tested: Comprehension _____ Vocabulary _____

Progress: Comprehension _____ Vocabulary _____

Activity 11–5
Summing It Up

Reflect now on all the activities you have done in this worktext and how you benefited from each. On a separate sheet of paper, create the following charts, mark the columns appropriately, and answer the questions at the end of each section.

Units Covered

Unit	very interesting	helpful	not helpful	poor	omit
Developing Study Skills					
Note Taking					
Taking Tests					
Improving Your Understanding					
Increasing Speed					
Skimming and Scanning					
Using the Dictionary					
Exploring the Library/ Media Center					
Reading for Enjoyment					

1. Which of the units did you *enjoy most*, and why?

2. Which of the units did you *benefit most from*, and why?

3. Which of the units did you *like least*, and why?

Reading Speed and Comprehension Activities

Type	very interesting	helpful	not helpful	poor	omit
Rapid discrimination					
Comprehension					
Speed-reading					

    1. Which of the activities did you *enjoy most*, and why?

    2. Which of the activities did you *benefit most from*, and why?

    3. Which of the activities did you *like least*, and why?

Study Skills Covered

Skill	very interesting	helpful	not helpful	poor	omit
Previewing your text					
Study setting					
Controlling your time					
Sizing up your instructor					
SQ3R					
Note-taking techniques					
Streamlining notes					
Memory					
Preparing for tests					
Test-taking anxiety					
Taking tests					

    1. Which of the skills did you *enjoy most*, and why?

    2. Which of the skills did you *benefit most from*, and why?

    3. Which of the skills did you *like least*, and why?

Now you have a composite picture of what you have gained from taking this class. Keep your worktext and notes to refer to—they will help you with your reading rate and comprehension, provide you with test-taking strategies, and more. The skills you've learned are valid now, while you are a student in the classroom, and years from now, as you train for a new job. As a student, as an employee, as an adult, you'll have many opportunities to apply what you've learned in this class.

Glossary

Almanac   volumes published annually that summarize the previous year's events.

A.P.   the abbreviation for *Associated Press*, a well-known news agency.

Banner headline   a headline that stretches across a newspaper page from one side to the other.

Byline   a line listing the author of the article.

Call numbers   numbers and letters indicating classifications of nonfiction books which determine the books' positions on library shelves.

Caption   the line beneath or beside a photograph or illustration providing information about it.

Card catalog   a filing system consisting of alphabetically arranged cards bearing the call numbers of each book in the library/media center.

Cloze   from the word *closure*; meaning to bring completion to a sentence.

Comfortable reading rate   the rate preferred by the reader.

Compare   to give both the similarities and the differences; a term used in essay questions.

Comprehension   the ability to understand what is read and pick out the most important ideas or facts.

Contrast   to give the differences only; a term used in essay questions.

Cramming   studying only the night before a test.

Criticize   to give a judgment or opinion based on reasons; good and bad points should be included; a term used in essay questions.

Dateline   a line indicating where the newspaper story action took place.

Day's high   the highest price a stock reached on a given day.

Day's low   the lowest price a stock reached on a given day.

Define   to give meanings but no details; often a matter of giving a memorized definition; a term used in essay questions.

Describe   to give details or a verbal picture of the topic; a term used in essay questions.

Dewey decimal system   a method of classifying nonfiction; it uses numbers to identify ten major subject categories.

Diacritical marks dots, dashes, and other symbols that show correct pronunciation of a word.

Diagram to include a chart, graph, or geometric drawing with labels and a brief explanation, if needed; a term used in essay questions.

Discuss to give reasons pro and con with details; a term used in essay questions.

Etymology the origin of a word.

Fiction writing that is based on imagination—that is not true; novels and short stories arranged alphabetically by the author's last name.

Fixation in reading, a pause of the eyes to take in words

Full signals obvious word "flags" such as *the first, the second, the third,* and so on.

Gist the central or main idea.

Guide words the words at the top of a dictionary page indicating the first and last entries on the page.

Half signals less obvious word "flags" such as *the next, the last, in summary,* and so on.

Headline large bold type above a newspaper article indicating the content of the story.

Highlighter a marker that allows print to show through; used in note taking to identify key information. When used with textbooks, the books must be student-owned.

Homograph words that have the same spelling but different meanings and origins.

Inferences sentence(s) in which the meaning is not directly stated.

Inflected form changes in the spelling of a word due to a tense change or a plural form.

Infotrac a library system that consists of a computer and a compact disk; it lists available material for specific topics.

Justify to prove or give reasons; a term used in essay questions.

Key words important words in a sentence.

Lead the first paragraph of a well-written story which answers the questions *who, what, when, where,* and *why* (the five Ws)

List to write a numbered list of words, sentences, or comments; a term used in essay questions.

Listing a form of note taking that uses main headings and lists to record information succinctly.

Jump a line stating that an article is continued on another page.

Last price the price at which a stock was selling when the market closed that day.

Library of Congress a method of classifying nonfiction; it uses letters to identify twenty-one major categories.

Main entry the word you look up in the dictionary.

Main idea the point the author is trying to make.

Margin notes a form of note taking in which key points are written in the margin. When used with textbooks, the books must be student-owned.

Microforms information from newspapers and magazines that has been photographed and reduced in size to be stored on microfiche or microfilm.

Net change the difference between a stock's last price on a given day and its last price on the previous day.

News agency an organization that sends news stories by wire. Two well-known news agencies are the Associated Press and United Press International.

Nonfiction   material that is true; all books that are not novels or short stories; nonfiction is classified using either the Dewey decimal or Library of Congress classification system.

NYSE   the abbreviation for the New York Stock Exchange; one of the major stock exchanges.

Outline   a system of note taking that involves recording main ideas and supporting details in a concise manner.

Overview   a comprehensive view of all the material; usually it is not followed by another reading.

Parts of speech   italic type in the dictionary indicating whether a word is a noun, pronoun, verb, adverb, and so on.

Patterning   a form of note taking that uses drawings, diagrams, charts, graphs, and so on.

Periodicals   newspapers, magazines, and digests that are published periodically.

Preview   a form of skimming; a view of the material before actually beginning to read; usually followed by a more thorough reading.

Push reading rate   a rate at which the reader sacrifices comfort to read as quickly as possible without diminishing comprehension.

Reading rate   the speed at which material is read.

Readers' Guide   *Readers' Guide to Periodical Literature;* a reference book that indexes articles on specific subjects.

Reference books   books such as dictionaries, encyclopedias, almanacs, and so on that are valuable sources of information for researchers.

Review   a form of skimming; to view the material again; it follows a previous reading.

Scan   to glance at a selection for specific information; not a true reading rate.

Sequence   arranging items in their proper order.

Signal words   word "flags" that indicate main points within sentences or paragraphs.

Skim   to pass quickly over an entire selection to get a general idea of its contents; not a true reading rate.

SQ3R   a study technique that uses the steps of survey, question, read, recite, and review to aid comprehension and retention.

Summarize   to give a brief, condensed account of the main ideas; omit details; a term used in essay questions.

Syllabication   division of a word into syllables.

Test anxiety   nervousness prior to taking a test.

Trace   to include details, progress, or history of a topic from beginning to end; a term used in essay questions.

Underlining   a method of note taking in which a student underlines key information as he or she reads. When used with textbooks, the books must be student-owned.

U.P.I.   the abbreviation for *United Press International,* a well-known news agency.

Variants   two or more correct spellings of a single word.

Verbal clues   like signal words; they "flag" what a lecturer thinks is important and may include on a test.

Vertical file   filing cabinets used in libraries for storage of small pamphlets, booklets, catalogs, and clippings on a variety of topics.

Words per minute (wpm)   the number of words read in one minute.

Year's high   the highest price a stock reached in one year's time.

Year's low   the lowest price a stock reached in one year's time.

Index

Alphabetizing, 132–34

Articles, recognizing main ideas in, 59–61

Book reports and projects
  creative, 181–82
  selecting a book, 180–81
  traditional, 183

Call numbers, 147–50

Card catalog, 150–52

Cause and effect relationships, 67–70
  analyzing, 69–70
  identifying, 67–69

Character development, 64–65
  background information, 66–67
  understanding, 64–65
  visualizing, 65–66

Classification of books
  fiction, 146–47
  nonfiction, 147–49
  using Dewey decimal system, 149–50
  using titles, 149

Classified ads, 170–72

Cloze, 72–73

Comprehension. *See* Reading comprehension

Concentration, 9–10

Conclusions, drawing, 71
  and cloze, 72

Dewey decimal system, 147–50

Diacritical marks, 140–41

Dictionaries
  alphabetical order, 132–34
  components of, 137
  diacritical marks, 140–41
  etymologies, 138–39
  terms and definitions, 134–37
  using all information in, 141–42
  using entry information in, 139–40

Editorial pages, 169–70

Etymologies, 136, 138–39

Fiction, 146–47

Front page, of newspaper, 169

Full signals, 27

Half signals, 27

Head movement, while reading, 97

Highlighting, 29

Homographs, 143–44

Inferences, 71

Instructor, determining expectations of, 14–15

Interest inventory, 4–5

Key words, 57

Library of Congress system, 147–48

Listing, in notes, 28

Magazines, 179–80

Main ideas, recognizing
  finding key words, 57
  in an article, 59–61
  in a paragraph, 58–59

Margin notes, 29

Memory, 35–36

Newspapers, 164–78
  classified ads, 170–72
  editorial pages, 169–70
  front page, 169
  jargon, 165–66
  sports section, 172–73
  stock quotations, 176–78
  weather pages, 174–76

Nonfiction, 147–48
  call numbers for, 148–49

Note taking, 20–33
  evaluating your present system, 20–21
  highlighting, 29
  listing, 28

margin notes, 29
outlining, 22–27
patterning, 27
signal words, 27
streamlining, 29–30

Outlining, 22–27
basics of, 22–24

Paragraphs, recognizing main ideas
in, 58–59
Patterning, 27
Periodical indexes, 154–57
Pointing, while reading, 97
Previewing, 6–8

*Readers' Guide to Periodical
Literature,* 157
Reading assessment, 5
Reading comprehension. *See also*
Reading rate, Reading speed
definition of, 93
evaluating skills, 83–99
and reading habits, 96–98
and reading rate, 93–94
and reading speed, 78, 79, 90
and vocabulary, 98–99
Reading for pleasure, 164–85
Reading habits, 96–98
head movement, 97
pointing, 97

subvocalizing, 97
vocalizing, 96
Reading rate. *See also* Reading
comprehension, Reading
speed
average, 113–16
flexible, 104–6
personal, 108
rapid, 117–19
recording your, 108–9, 120
slow and careful, 110–13
very rapid, 119
Reading speed. *See also* Reading
comprehension, Reading
rate
and comprehension, 78–79
increasing, 79–92
rapid discrimination drills,
79–89
speed and comprehension
drills, 93–99
timed readings, 90–92
and vocabulary, 98–99
Reference materials, 153–54
Research, 157–60

Scanning. *See* Skimming and
scanning
Sequencing, 61–69
Signal words, 27
Skimming and scanning, 104,
106–7, 121–29

Speed. *See* Reading rate, Reading
speed
Sports pages, 172–73
SQ3R method, 15–17
definition of, 16–17
Stock quotations, understanding,
176–78
Streamlining notes, 29–30
Study setting, 9–11
Subvocalizing, 97

Test anxiety, 40–43
Test taking, 34–55
and memory, 35–36
preparation, 37–39
reviewing, 51–52
strategies, 43–46
terminology, 51
tricks, 46–51
Time, 11
budgeting, 13
controlling, 12–13
tracking, 11–12

Vocalizing, 96

Weather pages, 174–76